Something Happened at the Library

Adding Song and Dance to Children's Story Programs

Rob Reid

American Library Association
Chicago   2007

The paper used in this publication meets the minimum requirements of American National Standard for Information Sciences—Permanence of Paper for Printed Library Materials, ANSI Z39.48-1992.⊚

Printed on 50-pound white offset, a pH-neutral stock, and bound in 10-point coated cover stock by Victor Graphics.

Library of Congress Cataloging-in-Publication Data
Reid, Rob.
 Something musical happened at the library : adding song and dance to children's story programs / Rob Reid.
  p.   cm.
 Includes bibliographical references and index.
 ISBN-13: 978-0-8389-0942-3 (alk. paper)
 ISBN-10: 0-8389-0942-6
 1. Children's libraries—Activity programs. 2. Children's songs—Discography. 3. Children—Books and reading. 4. Children's literature—Study and teaching (Elementary)—Activity programs. 5. Storytelling. 6. Dance. I. Title.
 Z718.1.R345 2007
 027.62'5—dc22   2007008586

ISBN-13: 978-0-8389-0942-3
ISBN-10: 0-8389-0942-6

Printed in the United States of America

11 10 09 08 07   5 4 3 2 1

Dedicated to the musical Freij Christiansen family—
Jim, Jenna, Andy, Michael, and Hannah

Contents

The Best Picture Books Featuring Music in Your Library 80

Preface

Something Musical Happened at the Library is a companion book to *Children's Jukebox*, second edition (ALA Editions, 2007). It was designed to share children's music ideas with public and school librarians, elementary school classroom teachers, music teachers, music therapists, camp counselors, scout leaders, parents, and anyone else who works and lives with children. It is intended for both nonmusicians and folks who have different levels of musical skill.

The first edition of *Children's Jukebox* (ALA Editions, 1995) was both a subject index of children's recorded music and a smorgasbord of children's music programming ideas. In the twelve years since that book came out, the children's music industry has grown—enough so that there are plenty of songs to index and a wealth of musical ideas to share in two books.

Children's musical recordings are often overlooked by librarians and teachers when developing story programs and classroom activities. I hope that the programming ideas found in the first part of the book are practical and inspire you to discover and develop more ideas to share with children. I hope that the second part of the book will help you to discover a wonderful assortment of children's picture books that deal with music and dance. May the children's book publishing industry keep them coming.

And I hope that all libraries and classrooms are filled with young voices singing and playing musical instruments on a regular basis.

Acknowledgments

I would like to thank the incredibly supportive staff at ALA Editions, particularly Laura Pelehach, Patrick Hogan, and Catherine English, for making me feel so special. We're close to achieving our "rainbow."

I would also like to thank the circulation staff at the L. E. Phillips Memorial Public Library in Eau Claire for handling my daily and weighty interlibrary loan requests with constant smiles. I also doff my hat to all of the libraries in the Indianhead Federated Library System (IFLS) as well as the staff at IFLS headquarters.

I couldn't have written this book or *Children's Jukebox*, second edition, without the support from all of the children's artists who generously donated their recordings and, more important, shared their talents with all of us.

Finally, thanks to my family—Jayne, Julia, Alice, Sam, Laura, and Steven—for your love, your support, and your nimble dodging of stacks of compact discs scattered throughout the house.

The author gratefully thanks the following artists for permission to reprint the lyrics to the following songs:

"Bluebird." Songwriters—Lisa Matthews and Mikel Gehl. Milkshake website: www.milkshakemusic.com. Address: P.O. Box 4864, Baltimore, MD 21211.

"Goodbye" by Yosi Levin. Website: www.yosimusic.com; children's music blog Indie Kids Rock: http://indiekidsrock.blogspot.com.

"The Hippopotamus Song." Words and music by Eric Ode from the recording *I Love My Shoes* produced by Deep Rooted Music, LLC. Website: www.ericode.com. Address: P.O. Box 1324, Sumner, WA 98390. Phone: 253-826-2115.

"Howdy Song" by Monty Harper. Website: www.montyharper.com. Phone: 405-624-3805.

"If Animals Could Dance" by The Learning Station. Website: www.learning stationmusic.com. Phone: 800-789-9990.

"List of Dances" by Jim Gill. Website: www.jimgill.com. Address: P.O. Box 2263, Oak Park, IL 60303-2263.

"Me, Myself and I" written by Kim Duncan for North Corner Music Group/ASCAP ©2005. Performed by Kim Duncan as Kimmy Schwimmy. Website: www.kimmyschwimmy.com.

"Moose" by the Banana Slug String Band. Website: www.bananaslugstringband .com. Address: P.O. Box 2262, Santa Cruz, CA 95063. Phone: 888-32-SLUGS (888-327-5847).

"A New Way to Say Hello" by Big Jeff DeSmedt. Big Jeff Music LLC. Website: www.bigjeffmusic.com.

"Oh, How Delicious Are Hot Tamales." Words and music by Sarah Barchas. ©1991 Sarah Barchas DBA High Haven Music. Reproduced by permission. Website: www.highhavenmusic.com.

"She'll Be Comin' 'round the Mountain," with new lyrics by Dana Cohenour, SwiggleDitties Entertainment. ©1995 Dana Cohenour. Website: www .swiggleditties.com. Address: P.O. Box 1958, Blaine, WA 98231. Phone: 800-557-3262.

"Super Mom." Words and music by Eric Nagler and Diane Buckley. Snagglepuss Music. Website: www.ericnagler.com.

"Wake Up, Toes" by Uncle Ruthie Buell, author, singer, songwriter, broadcaster.

"We're Going on a Picnic," lyrics by Sammie Haynes. Website: www .sammiehaynes.com.

Musical Story Program Lesson Plans

The following eight story program lesson plans feature a mix of songs and picture storybooks. Each lesson plan is designed to be approximately thirty minutes in length. They all begin with an overview of the program—"Program at a Glance"—and a recommended theme-related opening song to set the atmosphere as the audience gets settled. A different "hello song" is used for each program, and many of these are generic enough that they can be switched from one program to another. The lesson plans follow a mix of picture books and songs before ending with a "good-bye song." These "good-bye songs" can also be switched from program to program. Note that most picture books don't need to be about music or dance to work in musical story programs. At the time of this writing, every recording and book listed in the story program lesson plans was available for purchase.

More programming ideas appear following the story program lesson plans. These ideas are grouped under the headings of "Fun Pairings: Matching Children's Songs with Picture Books," "More Musical Ideas," "Call-and-Response Songs," "Cumulative Songs," and "Songs Sung in Rounds."

Enjoy!

ANIMAL FAIR
Program at a Glance

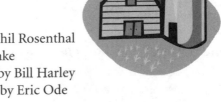

Opening Song: "Animal Fair" by Phil Rosenthal
Hello Song: "Bluebird" by Milkshake
Picture Book: *Sittin' Down to Eat* by Bill Harley
Song: "The Hippopotamus Song" by Eric Ode

♪ 1 ♪

Picture Book: *If You Give a Moose a Muffin* by Laura Joffe Numeroff
Song: "Moose" by the Banana Slug String Band
Song/Puppet Show: "Place in the Choir" by Bill Staines
Picture Book: *If You Had a Nose like an Elephant's Trunk* by Marion Dane Bauer
Song: "Ants in My Pants" by Joe Scruggs
Good-bye Song: "See Ya Later, Alligator" by Stephen Fite

Preparation and Presentation
Opening Song

"Animal Fair" from the recording *Animal Songs* by Phil Rosenthal (American Melody, 1996).

Play a recording of the popular song "Animal Fair" as the children enter the story program area. This traditional song can also be found on the following recordings:

> Beall, Pamela, and Susan Nipp. *Wee Sing Silly Songs*. Price Stern Sloan, 1982.
>
> Berkner, Laurie. *Whaddaya Think of That?* Two Tomatoes, 2000.
>
> Muldaur, Maria. *Swingin' in the Rain*. Music for Little People, 1998.
>
> Roth, Kevin. *Travel Song Sing Alongs*. Marlboro, 1994.

There is a pop-up picture-book version of "Animal Fair" by Anthony Browne (Candlewick, 2002). Have a copy available for the early arrivals to look through. You may wish to post the lyrics on a wall in case older children and adults want to sing along.

> I went to the animal fair,
> The birds and beasts were there,
> The big baboon by the light of the moon
> Was combing his auburn hair.
> The monkey bumped the skunk,
> And sat on the elephant's trunk,
> The elephant sneezed and fell to his knees
> And that was the end of the monk,
> The monk, the monk, the monk,
> The monk, the monk, the monk.

Hello Song

"Bluebird" from the recording *Bottle of Sunshine* by Milkshake (Milkshake, 2004).

Sing this simple tune or play the recording to welcome the children to the program.

1. Bluebird, bluebird, singing me a new song,
   Bluebird, bluebird, hello to you.
   Red bird, red bird, building up a new nest,
   Red bird, red bird, hello to you.

Chorus:
Hello to all the flowers in the garden,
Hello to all the fish in the pond.
Hello to all the trees in the forest,
Hello to you and me.

2. Ladybug, ladybug, crawling on my finger,
   Ladybug, ladybug, hello to you.
   Chipmunk, chipmunk, chewing on a chestnut,
   Chipmunk, chipmunk, hello to you.

(Chorus)

3. Little friend, little friend, coming out to play now,
   Little friend, little friend, hello to you.
   Bluebird, bluebird, singing me a new song,
   Bluebird, bluebird, hello to you.

You can even add new verses following the pattern of the lyrics. For example:

Children, children, welcome to story time,
Children, children, hello to you.

Picture Book

Sittin' Down to Eat by Bill Harley, illustrated by Kitty Harvill (August House, 1996).

Read this picture book based on the popular Harley song about a group of large animals that squeezes into a boy's home. The house finally explodes with a "BOOM!" when a caterpillar crawls in. In the endnotes, Harley advises the reader to simply read the lyrical text, pay attention to the natural rhythms in the verse, and play around with the animal noises. For those musically inclined storytellers who prefer to sing the text, the complete score of "Sittin' Down to Eat" can be found in the book *Do It Together: A Collection of Favorite Songs* by Bill Harley (Hal Leonard, 2006).

Recordings of the song can be found on

Harley, Bill. *Big Big World*. A&M, 1993.

Harley, Bill. *Play It Again*. Round River, 1999.

Song

"The Hippopotamus Song" from the recording *I Love My Shoes* by Eric Ode (Deep Rooted, 2005).

Since one of the animals that visits the boy in "Sittin' Down to Eat" is a hippopotamus, make that connection clear to the audience as an introduction to this fun, cumulative, sound-effects song. This is an enjoyable song to have the audience join in as the recording is played. Ode has hand movements for the song on his website: www.ericode.com.

1. Stompin' through the jungle is the hippopotamus. Boom! Boom! (2x)
   With sandpaper skin from top to bottomus,
   Oh, how I love that hippopotamus. Boom! Boom!

2. Swimmin' in the river is the hippopotamus. Splish, splash, Boom! Boom! (2x)
   With sandpaper skin from top to bottomus,
   Oh, how I love that hippopotamus. Splish, splash, Boom! Boom!

3. Chasing all the monkeys is the hippopotamus. Eee, eee, splish, splash, Boom! Boom! . . .

4. Eating all the mangoes is the hippopotamus. Munch, munch, eee, eee, splish, splash, Boom! Boom! . . .

5. Sleeping in the jungle is the hippopotamus. Snore, snore, munch, munch, eee, eee, splish, splash, Boom! Boom!

Picture Book

If You Give a Moose a Muffin by Laura Joffe Numeroff, illustrated by Felicia Bond (HarperCollins, 1991).

"If you give a moose a muffin, he'll want some jam to go with it." A child invites a moose into the house, and one thing leads to another. Soon the moose is making an elaborate puppet show. The moose sees some blackberries, which remind him of jam. "And chances are, if you give him the jam, he'll want a muffin to go with it."

Song

"Moose" from the recording *Penguin Parade* by the Banana Slug String Band (Music for Little People, 1995).

Play the recording and add the following motions to these lyrics:

> I have antlers (*splay hands over head like antlers*)
> And a nose (*point to nose*)
> I have hooves for toes (*hold up one foot*)
> And I stand about six feet tall (*stretch hand overhead—even if you're six feet or taller*)
> I'm in the mud up to my knees (*draw an imaginary line across your knees*)
> Just a-chewin' on the leaves (*make a chewing motion*)
> I'm a moose, moose, can't you hear me call? (*point to self*)

On the recording, the band sings it again, bellowing like a moose, then softer, and then again in a whisper, and "one last time for all the 'mooses' in Maine, Manitoba, Michigan, Minnesota, Montana, and Miami (Miami?)."

Song/Puppet Show

"Place in the Choir" from the recording *The Happy Wanderer* by Bill Staines (Red House, 1993).

If you have several animal puppets, pass them out to the children and have them make their puppets "sing" along with the recording. "Place in the Choir" can also be found on the following recordings:

Abell, Timmy. *The Farmer's Market*. Upstream, 1989.

Grammer, Red. *Down the Do-Re-Mi*. Red Note, 1991.

Knight, Tom. *Don't Kiss a Codfish/When I Grow Up*. Tom Knight, 2005.

The song can also be found under the title "All God's Critters" on the following recording:

McCutcheon, John. *Howjadoo*. Rounder, 1986.

The song is also found in picture-book format under the title *All God's Critters Got a Place in the Choir* by Bill Staines (Dutton, 1989).

Picture Book

If You Had a Nose like an Elephant's Trunk by Marion Dane Bauer (Holiday House, 2001).

Bauer takes a whimsical look at creatures' physical features and wonders what it would be like to have feet like a fly's ("you could walk up the wall"), a tail like a horse's ("you could brush the flies from your friends' faces"), or a mouth like a mosquito's ("you can get a sip of milk without ever opening a carton"). Bauer concludes that there are many things you can do with your own human features.

Song

"Ants in My Pants" from the recording *Late Last Night* by Joe Scruggs (Educational Graphics, 1984).

Simply play the recording and let Scruggs lead the listeners through an assortment of lively movements, such as the "OOOOH, There's a Snake Shimmy and Shake," the "Crocodile Rock," the "Twist and Turn, Wiggle Worm Squirm," and the title-inspired "I've Got the Ants in My Pants Dance."

Good-bye Song

"See Ya Later, Alligator" from the recording *Havin' Fun and Feelin' Groovy* by Stephen Fite (Melody House, 2001).

Simply end the program with a spoken "See ya later, alligator—after while, crocodile" and let the audience leave the program area while Fite's recording plays.

BON APPÉTIT

Program at a Glance

Opening Song: "Bon Appétit" by Cathy Fink and Marcy Marxer
Hello Song: "Way over There" by Colleen and Uncle Squaty
Picture Book: *Cactus Soup* by Eric Kimmel
Song: "Oh, How Delicious Are Hot Tamales" by Sarah Barchas
Picture Book: *Beverly Billingsly Takes the Cake* by Alexander Stadler
Song: "Stinky Cake" by Carole Peterson
Picture Book: *Hey, Pancakes!* by Tamson Weston
Song: "Flap Flapjacks" by Cathy Fink and Marcy Marxer
Picture Book: *Peanut Butter and Jelly* by Nadine Bernard Westcott
Song: "Peanut Butter 'n Jelly" by Magical Music Express
Good-bye Song: "Now It's Time to Say Goodbye" by Ralph's World

Preparation and Presentation
Opening Song

"Bon Appétit" from the recording *Bon Appétit!* by Cathy Fink and Marcy Marxer (Rounder, 2003).

As the audience members enter the program area, play the title song from this Grammy Award–winning recording. The song celebrates the food we get from farmers and fishermen. There are several opportunities to say "Bon appétit."

Hello Song

"Way over There" from the recording *1, 2, 3, Four-Ever Friends* by Colleen and Uncle Squaty (Colleen and Uncle Squaty, 1995).

Play this recording, which features many ways to say hello in foreign languages. The children will quickly learn to repeat these words. Have them point or wave whenever Colleen and Uncle Squaty sing "way over there."

Picture Book

Cactus Soup by Eric Kimmel, illustrated by Phil Huling (Marshall Cavendish, 2004).

In this retelling of the traditional story "Stone Soup," Mexican villagers hide their food when they see several soldiers approaching their little town. The soldiers trick the villagers into adding salt, peppers, chicken, onions, beans, carrots, and tomatoes into a soup that began with one cactus thorn and water. They add tortillas, tamales, chorizo, and more to the fiesta. The villagers learn that feeding soldiers is no problem "as long as we remember how to make . . . Cactus Soup!"

Song

"Oh, How Delicious Are Hot Tamales" from the recording *¡Piñata! and More* by Sarah Barchas (High Haven, 1997).

Play this pattern bilingual song as a follow-up to the book *Cactus Soup*. Teach the children the chorus and the line, "Yummy, yummy yum, crunch, crunch" before playing the recording.

1. Oh, how delicious are hot tamales,
   Hot tamales with chili verde.
   Ay que sabrosos son tamales picantes.
   Yummy, yummy yum, crunch, crunch.

2. Oh, how delicious are crispy tacos,
   Crispy tacos with lots of carne.
   Ay que sabrosos son taco dorados.
   Yummy, yummy yum, crunch, crunch.

Chorus:
Llena mi plato.
Fill up my plate.
I'm as hungry as I can be.
Llena mi plato.
Fill up my plate
With Mexican food for me.
Crunch, crunch!

3. Oh, how delicious are enchiladas,
   Enchiladas with lots of queso.
   Ay que sabrosas son enchiladas.
   Yummy, yummy yum, crunch, crunch.

4. Oh, how delicious are fresh tortillas,
   Fresh tortillas with lots of salsa.
   Ay que sabrosas son tortillas recién hechas.
   Yummy, yummy yum, crunch, crunch.

(Chorus)

5. Oh, how delicious are big tostadas,
   Big tostadas with lots of frijoles.
   Ay que sabrosas son tostadas grandes.
   Yummy, yummy yum, crunch, crunch.

6. Oh, how delicious are chimichangas,
   Chimichangas with guacamole.
   Ay que sabrosas son chimichangas.
   Yummy, yummy yum, crunch, crunch.

(Chorus)
Coda: Con comida Mexicana para mi. Crunch, crunch!

Picture Book

Beverly Billingsly Takes the Cake by Alexander Stadler (Harcourt, 2005).
    Beverly bakes a Caramel Candy Castle Cake with her mother. Unfortunately, she forgets to grease the pan, and the cake has to be cut into two pieces. Beverly

throws a tantrum until her mother shows her how the cake can be turned into a butterfly cake. Her friends ask her if she'll make cakes for their birthdays.

Song

"Stinky Cake" from the recording *Stinky Cake* by Carole Peterson (Macaroni Soup, 2005).

Tommy Patten wrote this simple ditty about adding weird items to the cake. The song starts with "We're going to make a stinky cake" and then asks the listeners what they might put into it. Peterson's version suggests adding dirty socks, moldy fish, and baby diapers. Ask the kids what disgusting things they would add to the stinky cake.

Picture Book

Hey, Pancakes! by Tamson Weston, illustrated by Stephen Gammell (Harcourt, 2003).

Three children celebrate their morning by making pancakes while their parents are still in bed. Gammell's wild pencil drawings capture the fun mess the three make. The children have special fun flipping the pancakes in the air, although some land on the dog. And possibly the most amazing thing in the entire book—the kids clean up after themselves.

Song

"Flap Flapjacks" from the recording *Scat like That* by Cathy Fink and Marcy Marxer (Rounder, 2005).

You can play the recording or simply challenge the kids to say the tongue-twisting phrases five times each. The food related tongue twisters include "flap flapjacks," "shredded Swiss cheese," and "double bubble gum." Fink and Marxer also sing the phrases "pink piggy bank," "knapsack straps," and "Sam's Sock Shop."

Picture Book

Peanut Butter and Jelly by Nadine Bernard Westcott (Dutton, 1987).

A chef enters a house and helps a little boy and girl bake a gigantic loaf of bread. He saws a slice (with a saw) as a group of elephants joins them. The elephants crack and mash the peanuts to make peanut butter. They roll in a bathtub filled with grapes to make jelly. Everyone finally assembles a table-sized peanut butter and jelly sandwich. Sing the book or show the pictures and listen to the hilarious version in the recording below by Magical Music Express.

Song

"Peanut Butter 'n Jelly" from the recording *Music Is Magic* by Magical Music Express (Magical Music Express, 2002).

Pam Donkin and Greta Pedersen, who make up the duo Magical Music Express, sing the traditional version of the song with a little extra enthusiasm with the help of lively kids.

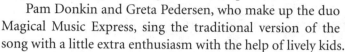

1. Oh, peanut butter and jelly (2x).

   First you take the peanuts and you smash 'em, you smash 'em, you smash 'em, smash 'em, smash 'em.

2. Oh, peanut butter and jelly (2x).

   First you take the peanuts and you smash 'em, you smash 'em, you smash 'em, smash 'em, smash 'em.

   Then you take the berries and you mush 'em, you mush 'em, you mush 'em, mush 'em, mush 'em.

3. Oh, peanut butter and jelly (2x).

   First you take the peanuts and you smash 'em, you smash 'em, you smash 'em, smash 'em, smash 'em.

   Then you take the berries and you mush 'em, you mush 'em, you mush 'em, mush 'em, mush 'em.

   Then you take the bread and you spread it, you spread it, you spread it, spread it, spread it.

4. Oh, peanut butter and jelly (2x).

   First you take the peanuts and you smash 'em, you smash 'em, you smash 'em, smash 'em, smash 'em.

   Then you take the berries and you mush 'em, you mush 'em, you mush 'em, mush 'em, mush 'em.

   Then you take the bread and you spread it, you spread it, you spread it, spread it, spread it.

   Then you take the sandwich and you eat it, you eat it, you eat it, eat it, eat it.

5. *(Say the following verse as if you have a mouthful of peanut butter.)*

   Oh, peanut butter and jelly (2x).

   First you take the peanuts and you smash 'em, you smash 'em, you smash 'em, smash 'em, smash 'em.

   Then you take the berries and you mush 'em, you mush 'em, you mush 'em, mush 'em, mush 'em.

   Then you take the bread and you spread it, you spread it, you spread it, spread it, spread it.

Then you take the sandwich and you *(make a swallowing noise and sing in a normal voice)* eat it, you eat it, you eat it, eat it, eat it.

6. *(Sing the entire verse one more time in a clear singing voice.)*
Oh, peanut butter and jelly (2x).
First you take the peanuts and you smash 'em, you smash 'em, you smash 'em, smash 'em, smash 'em.
Then you take the berries and you mush 'em, you mush 'em, you mush 'em, mush 'em, mush 'em.
Then you take the bread and you spread it, you spread it, you spread it, spread it, spread it.
Then you take the sandwich and you eat it, you eat it, you eat it, eat it, eat it.

Good-bye Song

"Now It's Time to Say Goodbye" from the recording *Ralph's World* by Ralph's World (Mini Fresh, 2001).

This extremely simple good-bye tune tells everyone that it's now time to say good-bye and may happiness follow you everywhere.

BOOGIE-WOOGIE BARNYARD

Program at a Glance

Opening Song: "Music Farm" by Xtatik
Hello Song: "When Cows Get Up in the Morning"
Picture Book: *Dooby Dooby Moo* by Doreen Cronin
Song: "Twinkle, Twinkle in Cow," adapted by Rob Reid
Picture Book: *Punk Farm* by Jarrett J. Krosoczka
Song: "Goofy Old MacDonald" by Carole Peterson
Picture Book: *Young MacDonald* by David Milgrim
Picture Book: *Cows in the Kitchen* by June Crebbin
Picture Book: *Skip to My Lou* by Nadine Bernard Westcott
Good-bye Song: "When Cows Go to Bed in the Evening," adapted by Rob Reid

Preparation and Presentation
Opening Song

"Music Farm" from the recording *World Playground 2* (Putumayo, 2001).

The artist Xtatik has a funky Caribbean farm song with "E-I-E-I-O" scattered throughout the song. Set the atmosphere by playing the recording as audience members enter the story program area.

Hello Song

"When Cows Get Up in the Morning." Traditional.

I learned this extremely simple traditional pattern song years ago and have used it with hundreds of children. "When cows get up in the morning, they always say 'Good day!' 'Moo, moo,' that's how they say 'Good day!'" Deliver the song in an energetic manner. You can do it as a call-and-response song as well as a sound-effects song. Ask the children to think of other animals and their sounds. The tune can be found under the title "Say Good Day" on the recording *Tiny Tunes* by Carole Peterson (Macaroni Soup, 2005).

Picture Book

Dooby Dooby Moo by Doreen Cronin, illustrated by Betsy Lewin (Atheneum, 2006).

The characters from Cronin's popular Click, Clack, Moo farm books are back and putting on a talent show in the barn. First prize is a trampoline. The cows sing "Twinkle, Twinkle, Little Star," the sheep sing "Home on the Range," and the pigs do an interpretive dance. The duck jumps onstage at the last minute and quacks "Born to Be Wild." We don't know exactly who wins the contest, but all of the animals can be seen jumping on the trampoline at the end of the book.

Song

"Twinkle, Twinkle in Cow," adapted by Rob Reid.

Follow up the talents displayed in the Cronin book with your own reenactment. Instruct your audience members to sing "Twinkle, Twinkle, Little Star" by mooing the words. "Moo moo moo moo moo moo moo . . ." Once they finish that song, they can next "baa" to the tune of "Home on the Range." (And if you have any adventurous adults in the audience, they might want to try their hand at quacking "Born to Be Wild.")

Picture Book

Punk Farm by Jarrett J. Krosoczka (Knopf, 2005).

This hilarious book features a sheep singing lead vocals for a barnyard band. A goat plays the bass guitar, a pig plays lead guitar, a chicken plucks the keyboards, and a cow bangs away at the drums. The sheep sings their hit song to the tune of "Old MacDonald Had a Farm" and ends with a rousing "Thank you Wisconsin!" This was my pick for the 2005 Robbie Award for the funniest children's book of the year. The website, www.punkfarm.com, has a downloadable version of the song.

Song

"Goofy Old MacDonald" from the recording *Tiny Tunes* by Carole Peterson (Macaroni Soup, 2005).

Peterson does a nice job modeling silly interactions with her audience while singing "Old MacDonald Had a Farm." Peterson energetically sings the wrong animal sounds and lets the children correct her. Listen to her recording and give a similar try with your own giggling audience.

Picture Book

Young MacDonald by David Milgrim (Dutton, 2006).

Young MacDonald creates weird hybrid animals on his farm. He combines a pig with a horse to create "a Hig." This new creature says, "With an oink-neigh here / And an oink-neigh there." The inventive farmer goes on to create "some Deese" (ducks and geese), "a Shicken," (sheep and chickens), "some Mucks" (mice and ducks), and more. He accidentally creates "a Bog," a boy and a dog, before setting things right. Sing the entire text.

Picture Book

Cows in the Kitchen by June Crebbin, illustrated by Katharine McEwen (Scholastic, 1998).

Here's another picture book where you can sing the entire text—this time to the tune of "Skip to My Lou." "Cows in the kitchen, moo, moo, moo. . . . That's what we do, Tom Farmer!" Several cows are seen trashing the farmhouse kitchen. Several other animals invade the house. Pigs are in the pantry, sheep are on the sofa, and more. Where's Tom Farmer? Asleep in the haystack. The kids will sing along, especially with the animal noises. Fran Avni recorded this song on her recording *Little Ears: Songs for Reading Readiness* (Leapfrog School House, 2000).

Picture Book

Skip to My Lou by Nadine Bernard Westcott (Little, Brown, 1989).

If the audience is willing to sing one more time, share this short picture-book version of the traditional song. Westcott sets the book on a farm with more barnyard animals invading the farmhouse, this time to the dismay of the farmer's son. He decides to join the animals in a big dance (after a splash in the bathtub). The boy and the animals clean up just in time before the parents return home. "Skip to my Lou, my darling! Phew!"

Good-bye Song

"When Cows Go to Bed in the Evening." Traditional, adapted by Rob Reid.

Take the same sound effects and tune from "When Cows Get Up in the Morning" and make a simple good-bye song. Ask the kids for more animal and noise ideas.

> When cows go to bed in the evening, they always say "Good night."
> "Moo, moo." That's how they say "Good night."
> (*Deliver the animal noises in a tired manner.*)

After singing a few farm-animal verses, close with

> When kids leave storytime, they always say "Good-bye."
> "See ya! Bye-bye." That's how they say "Good-bye."

Solicit other ways to say "good-bye" from the kids before they leave.

FAMILY TREE
Program at a Glance

Opening Song: "Family Tree" by Tom Chapin
Hello Song: "A New Way to Say Hello" by Big Jeff
Picture Book: *The Family Book* by Todd Parr
Song: "The Couch Potato Pokey" by Jean Feldman
Picture Book: *What Moms Can't Do* by Douglas Wood
Song: "Super Mom" by Eric Nagler
Picture Book: *What Dads Can't Do* by Douglas Wood
Song: "Super Dad" adapted by Rob Reid from Eric
    Nagler's song "Super Mom"
Picture Book: *My Family Plays Music* by Judy Cox
Song: "Mama Don't Allow" adapted by Rob Reid
Good-bye Song: "Family Goodbyes" by Jim Gill

Preparation and Presentation
Opening Song

"Family Tree" from the recording *Family Tree* by Tom Chapin (Sony, 1992).

Play this ode to family lineage as the audience members enter the program area. They may join in when Chapin sings the catchy line, "We're a family and we're a tree."

Hello Song

"A New Way to Say Hello" from the recording *Big Jeff* by Big Jeff (Big Jeff, 2000).
Act out the motions as Big Jeff sings:

1. Ba-dum dum dum, I know a new way
   to say hello,
   Say hello, say hello.
   I know a new way to say hello,
   All you do is *blink your eyes.*

2. Ba-dum dum dum, I know a new way
   to say hello,
   Say hello, say hello.
   I know a new way to say hello,
   All you do is *wiggle your ears.*

3. Ba-dum dum dum, I know a new way
   to say hello,
   Say hello, say hello.
   I know a new way to say hello,
   All you do is *stomp your feet.*
   Now make up your own!

4. Ba-dum dum dum, I know a new way
   to say hello,
   Say hello, say hello.
   I know a new way to say hello,
   All you do is . . . (*let the kids make up their own motions*)

5. But I still like the old way to say hello,
   Say hello, say hello,
   I still like the old way to say hello,
   All you do is *wave your hand!*

Picture Book

The Family Book by Todd Parr (Little, Brown, 2003).

I'm partial to Parr's colorful, simple picture books, which have subtle touches of humor. This book celebrates the diverse makeup of families today. Some families are large; some are small. Some families adopt children; some have "a stepmom or stepdad and stepsisters and stepbrothers." Some like to be noisy; some are quiet. "All families can help each other be strong!"

Song

"The Couch Potato Pokey" from the recording *Is Everybody Happy?* by Jean Feldman (Jean Feldman, 2000).

Jean Feldman, aka Dr. Jean, devised a clever adaptation of the traditional song "The Hokey Pokey." She uses minimal movements. Joke with your audience that "some" families like to sit around and watch television or movies together and that they need to be reminded to exercise. Dr. Jean leads everyone in moving their thumbs, noses, elbows, eyebrows, chins, and pinkies. Hilarious!

Picture Book

What Moms Can't Do by Douglas Wood, illustrated by Doug Cushman (Simon & Schuster, 2001).

The young narrator states that moms can't do many things that regular people can do. Moms "have trouble keeping things cleaned up," and when watching movies, "sometimes they need protection during the scary parts." Of course, the illustrations show the real story of the abilities of mothers.

Song

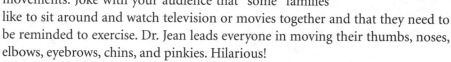

"Super Mom" from the recording *Improvise with Eric Nagler* by Eric Nagler (Rounder, 1989).

Follow Wood's picture book with this gyrating song that celebrates the superpowers that mothers possess.

   1. My mom says she's a Super Mom,
      But I don't think that's true.
      She washes the windows all day long
      But I can do that, too. (*make a washing motion with your right hand*)

   2. My mom says she's a Super Mom,
      But I don't think that's true.
      She works the computer and the telephone
      But I can do that, too. (*add the motions of pressing a computer keyboard with your left hand while miming talking on the phone as if the phone is tucked under your chin*)

   3. My mom says she's a Super Mom,
      But I don't think that's true.
      She bounces the baby on her hips
      But I can do that, too. (*add hip-swaying motions to the previous motions*)

4. My mom says she's a Super Mom,
     But I don't think that's true.
     She minds the kids and the dogs and the cat
     But I can do that, too. (*add the motion of nodding your head in three directions over and over*)

5. My mom says she's a Super Mom,
     But I don't think that's true.
     She jogs to the office every day
     But I can do that, too. (*run in place while doing all previous motions*)
     My mom says she's a Super Mom!!!

Picture Book

What Dads Can't Do by Douglas Wood, illustrated by Doug Cushman (Simon & Schuster, 2000).

Share this companion book to *What Moms Can't Do* as we learn that, unlike regular people, "dads can't pitch a baseball very hard" or win at checkers or even sleep in late. Of course, despite these flaws, "a dad never stops loving you." Wood and Cushman also give grandmothers, teachers, and even Santa similar treatment in their own Simon & Schuster picture books:

What Grandmas Can't Do (2005)

What Santa Can't Do (2004)

What Teachers Can't Do (2002)

Song

"Super Dad" adapted by Rob Reid from Eric Nagler's song "Super Mom."

Do similar gyrations as "Super Mom" but to the following words and motions:

1. My dad says he's a Super Dad,
     But I don't think that's true.
     He kicks the football down the field
     But I can do that, too. (*make a kicking motion with one foot*)

2. My dad says he's a Super Dad,
     But I don't think that's true.
     He pushes the swing all day long
     But I can do that, too. (*add the motion of pushing a swing with one hand*)

3. My dad says he's a Super Dad,
   But I don't think that's true.
   He plays peek-a-boo with the baby
   But I can do that, too. (*add the motion of placing the other hand over both eyes repeatedly*)

4. My dad says he's a Super Dad,
   But I don't think that's true.
   He gives us all a good-night kiss
   But I can do that, too. (*make several kisses in the air while doing the previous motions*)
   My dad says he's a Super Dad!!!

Picture Book

My Family Plays Music by Judy Cox, illustrated by Elbrite Brown (Holiday House, 2003).

A young percussionist belongs to a very musical family. Her mother plays the fiddle in a country-and-western band, her father plays cello in a string quartet, sister Emily plays clarinet in a marching band, and brother Paul plays guitar in a rock 'n' roll band. Other family members have their own musical specialties, including little niece Sadie banging away on pots and pans.

Song

"Mama Don't Allow." Traditional, adapted by Rob Reid.

Celebrate the Cox picture book by singing the popular, simple song "Mama Don't Allow," with the addition of shouting "Yes, she does!" after various verses.

1. Mama don't allow no fiddle playing 'round here (Yes, she does!).
   Mama don't allow no fiddle playing 'round here (Yes, she does!).
   We don't care what Mama don't allow,
   We're going to play the fiddle anyhow,
   Mama don't allow no fiddle playing 'round here (Yes, she does!).

Have everyone mime motions of playing the fiddle and then the motions of the instruments of the following verses, which parallel the Cox picture book:

2. Mama don't allow no cello playing 'round here . . . (*mime drawing a bow in front of your body*)
3. Mama don't allow no clarinet playing 'round here . . . (*mime playing the keys of a clarinet*)

4. Mama don't allow no guitar playing 'round here . . . (*strum an imaginary guitar*)

When you get to the final verse, halt everything and ask the audience, "What exactly will Mama allow? Percussion playing!" Pass out a variety of rhythm instruments, pots, pans, wooden spoons, blocks, whatever is on hand, and sing one more verse with the audience members banging along.

5. Mama DOES allow some percussion playing 'round here . . .

The song "Mama Don't Allow" can be found on the following recordings:

Arnold, Linda. *Happiness Cake*. Ariel, 1988.

Hullabaloo. *Sing Along with Sam*. Hullabaloo, 2006.

Old Town School of Folk Music. *Wiggleworms Love You*. Old Town School, 2005.

Rosenthal, Phil. *Folksongs and Bluegrass for Children*. Rounder, 2000.

Rymer, Brady. *Every Day Is a Birthday*. Bumblin' Bee, 2006.

The song can be found as the text to the picture book *Mama Don't Allow* by Thatcher Hurd (HarperCollins, 1984).

For an extra treat, watch sound-effects expert Fred Newman demonstrate how he plays all of the instruments with his mouth in the Reading Rainbow video segment featuring Hurd's picture book. The DVD is listed as "Mama Don't Allow" (episode 30) on the Reading Rainbow website: http://gpn.unl.edu/rainbow/.

Good-bye Song

"Family Goodbyes" from the recording *Moving Rhymes for Modern Times* by Jim Gill (Jim Gill, 2006).

Gill sings about the unusual ways his family waves good-bye. Play the recording and move the appropriate body part. Gill manages to include waving your foot, hair, thumb, nose, toe, lips, wrist, knee, chin, tongue, and ear.

MAY I HAVE THIS DANCE?
Program at a Glance

Opening Song: "Don't Make Me Dance" by Tom Chapin
Hello Song: "Hello" by Peter Alsop
Picture Book: *How Can You Dance?* by Rick Walton
Song: "List of Dances" by Jim Gill
Picture Book: *Lila Bloom* by Alexander Stadler

Picture Book: *Hilda Must Be Dancing* by Karma Wilson
Song: "If Animals Could Dance" by the Learning Station
Picture Book: *Baby Dance* by Ann Taylor
Good-bye Song: "I Had a Friend" by Laurie Berkner

Preparation and Presentation
Opening Song

"Don't Make Me Dance" from the recording *Some Assembly Required* by Tom Chapin (Razor & Tie, 2005).
   This funny tongue-twisting song will set the mood for this particularly active program. Play it as the audience gathers in the story program area.

Hello Song

"Hello" from the recording *Uh-Oh!* by Peter Alsop (Moose School, 2002).
   Play this recording and let the kids follow Alsop's directions as he celebrates the day. He expresses his happiness by dancing, singing, waving arms, slapping knees, scrunching noses, whispering, singing "up squeaky high," and more. The complete lyrics can be found on Alsop's website: www.peteralsop.com.

Picture Book

How Can You Dance? by Rick Walton, illustrated by Ana Lopez-Escriva (Putnam, 2001).
   Audience members can move around to the very creative dance directions given in the book. They will dance like "the king of the kangaroos," dance as if one foot is sore, dance as if they were swimming, and dance like a tree. They'll also be able to dance like their mother, a crab, a fox, the leader of a marching band, a bee, a donkey, and a snake. The final dance asks them to wave good-bye as they dance like a cloud drifting away.

Song

"List of Dances" from the recording *Jim Gill Makes It Noisy in Boise, Idaho* by Jim Gill (Jim Gill, 1995).
   Keep the children up on their feet and demonstrate their dance interpretations for sixteen more creative dances. Play the recording and let Gill lead the way. Don't worry if the children are stumped on how they should dance for some of the choices. Gill moves quickly from one dance to another.

   I made a list of all of the dances in this song,
   I made a list so that I'll never sing 'em wrong,

'Cause it's hard to remember and easy to forget
A list that is sixteen dances long.
You do the tall . . .
You do the small . . .
You do the hop . . .
And the stop!
You do the slow . . .
You do the tip-toe . . .
You do the curl . . .
And do the twirl.
You do the hide . . .
You do the slide . . .
You do the sleep . . .
And do the creep.
You do the slump . . .
You do the jump . . .
You do the sway . . .
And do the stay.
We've done dances like the tip-toe and the hop,
We've done them but it's still not time to stop,
'Cause though we danced it one time,
The list would seem brand new,
If we read it from the bottom to the top.

(*Reverse the order of the dances, starting with "the stay" and ending with "the tall."*)

Picture Book

Lila Bloom by Alexander Stadler (Farrar, Straus and Giroux, 2003).

The children will enjoy this brief break to sit and listen to a story about a young dancer who doesn't want to take ballet lessons anymore. Lila's aunt Celeste tells her to finish today's class, "and then you'll never have to go again." Madame Vera, the instructor, tells Lila that she's dancing like an old noodle and perhaps it's best that she's quitting. Lila is embarrassed and dances her best for the rest of the lesson. As she dances, Lila gets happier and decides to take "two classes a week instead of one."

Picture Book

Hilda Must Be Dancing by Karma Wilson, illustrated by Suzanne Watts (Margaret K. McElderry, 2004).

Hilda is a rather large hippopotamus that crashes throughout the jungle as she dances. The other animals try to distract Hilda from dancing. They suggest she take up knitting, but the yarn gets tangled. They encourage her to sing, but she "found she couldn't hold a tune." She finally discovers the joys of water ballet, which makes the jungle animals happy. The illustrations of Hilda dressed in her various dancing outfits are hilarious.

Song

"If Animals Could Dance" from the recording *La Di Da La Di Di Dance with Me* by the Learning Station (Monopoli/Learning Station, 2004).

Play the recording or sing the simple tune and encourage the children to move and sound like various animals.

> If animals could dance, they'd look so funny.
> A *cat* would dance and look just like this.
> And sound like this.
> And dance like this! And sound like this.

(*Replace "cat" with "cow," "dog," "duck," "elephant," "monkey," "rooster," "sheep," and "snake."*)

Picture Book

Baby Dance by Ann Taylor, illustrated by Marjorie van Heerden (HarperCollins, 1999).

A father swings his baby daughter back and forth and up and down while Mama is napping on the couch. The book starts with the lines "Hush little baby, don't you cry," and indeed, you can sing the entire text to the tune of "Hush Little Baby."

Good-bye Song

"I Had a Friend" from the recording *Buzz Buzz* by Laurie Berkner (Two Tomatoes, 1998).

Berkner rhymes people's names to describe the way they dance. For example, "I had a friend named Joni / And when she danced, she looked like bologna." You can pick out different names and rhyme them on the spot, using Berkner's song pattern. She ends the song with rhyming the name *Sly* with "and when he danced, he waved goodbye." Substitute any other name that rhymes with *good-bye* if you wish.

MORNING, NOON, AND NIGHT
Program at a Glance

Opening Song: "Blue Sparklin' Day" by Elizabeth McMahon
Hello Song: "Hello" by "Miss Jackie" Silberg

Picture Book: *Morning Song* by Mary McKenna Siddals
Song: "Wake Up, Toes" by Joanie Bartles
Picture Book: *Wake Up, City* by Susan Verlander
Picture Book: *Bing: Go Picnic* by Ted Dewan
Song: "We're Going on a Picnic" by Sammie Haynes
Picture Book: *Bats at the Beach* by Brian Lies
Picture Book: *Russell the Sheep* by Rob Scotton
Song: "Ten Sleepy Sheep" by Jessica Harper
Good-bye Song: "Wave Goodbye" by Colleen and Uncle Squaty

Preparation and Presentation
Opening Song

"Blue Sparklin' Day" from the recording *Blue Sparklin' Day* by Elizabeth McMahon (Rosie Rhubarb, 1993).

This program theme features a quick romp through a day's and night's events. As the audience enters the program area, play this happy-go-lucky, celebratory song.

Hello Song

"Hello" from the recording *Peanut Butter, Tarzan, and Roosters* by "Miss Jackie" Silberg (Miss Jackie, 1981).

This call-and-response song was written by Ella Jenkins. The singer sings out hello and inquires, "How are you?" The audience members respond that they are fine, and they hope the singer is, too. Silberg adds verses for waving hands, waving pinkie fingers in a quiet pinkie-finger voice, waving elbows, waving heads, waving tongues, shaking hands, and, finally, hugging.

Picture Book

Morning Song by Mary McKenna Siddals, illustrated by Elizabeth Sayles (Holt, 2001).

A little boy wakes up and says good morning to his blankie, his bear, and other familiar objects. He expresses sheer joy for the new morning, peek-a-booing at the sun, leaping around his room, and finally jumping into his father's arms. The boy also greets his eyes, nose, fingers, and toes, which leads nicely into the next song.

Song

"Wake Up, Toes" from the recording *Morning Magic* by Joanie Bartels (BMG, 1987).

This fun movement song was written by children's artist Uncle Ruthie. Have everyone wiggle the featured body part as it appears in the song.

1. Wake up toes, wake up toes,
   Wake up toes and wiggle, wiggle, wiggle.
   Wake up toes, wake up toes,
   Wake and wiggle in the morning.

2. Wake up feet . . .
3. Wake up legs . . .
4. Wake up arms . . .
5. Wake up hands . . .
6. Wake up head . . .
7. Wake up me (all of me) . . .

Picture Book

Wake Up, City by Susan Verlander (Chronicle Books, 2004).

An entire city goes through its morning routine with subways rumbling, shopkeepers opening their stores, newspapers being delivered, and more. This short, expressive book gets children thinking about all of the things they may do and encounter in a normal day. You may want to ask the audience to brainstorm a country version of this book and collect ideas about rural morning routines.

Picture Book

Bing: Go Picnic by Ted Dewan (David Fickling Books, 2005).

A picnic is an event one may partake of in the city or the country. This tiny, silly book follows a bunny named Bing and his friend Flop going on a picnic in a park. They proceed to add more and more items to the picnic basket (including a mobile phone). It starts to rain, so the two have their picnic indoors under a table.

Song

"We're Going on a Picnic" from the recording *Nature's ABCs* by Sammie Haynes (A Gentle Wind, 2004).

Play the short song for the kids and let them react to the singer's food choices. Let the kids brainstorm their own food choices, including silly food items. Write the ideas down and sing them aloud. Don't worry about making the lines rhyme.

We're going on a picnic, you and me,
Under the shade of the apple tree.

We've packed a picnic basket with our lunch
With lots of goodies for us to munch like:
Carrots and celery,
Peanut butter and jelly,
Tuna fish, hardboiled eggs,
Watermelon, lemonade,
Pretzels, potato chips,
Crackers, clam dip,
String cheese, cantaloupe,
Cherries, root beer float,
Pizza, pancakes,
Spaghetti, cornflakes,
Brownies, banana splits,
Cookies, chocolate chips,
Cotton candy, ice cream,
Fried dough, jelly beans,
Marshmallows, french fries,
Hot dogs, apple pie,
Earthworms, beetles,
Spiders, mosquitoes!
Ooooh! I'm not eating those!
But!
We're going on a picnic, you and me
Under the shade of the apple tree.
We've packed a picnic basket with our lunch
With lots of goodies for us to munch!
With lots of goodies for us to munch!

Picture Book

Bats at the Beach by Brian Lies (Houghton Mifflin, 2006).

As we move into the nighttime portion of the story program, we see that nocturnal creatures can also have picnics. Once the sun sets, some bats carry picnic supplies to a nearby beach. They play games, build sand castles, go surfing, sing around the campfire, and eat good food (such as pickled slugs and bug-mallows).

Picture Book

Russell the Sheep by Rob Scotton (HarperCollins, 2005).

Russell has a hard time falling asleep. He tries a variety of hilarious methods, such as taking off his wool (he got too cold) and counting stars (he reached six hundred million billion and ten—twice). He finally decides to count nine sheep—that doesn't work, either. However, once he counts the tenth sheep—himself—he falls asleep and doesn't even wake up with the other sheep in the morning.

Song

"Ten Sleepy Sheep" from the recording *40 Winks* by Jessica Harper (Alacazam, 1998).

Harper's counting-pattern song follows sheep on a hill. Each verse ends with the line "One for the money, two for the show / Three, let's go / Baa baa baa." Play the recording, and the kids will quickly join in and sing these lines. There's also a "baa baa" chorus that lends itself to audience participation.

Good-bye Song

"Wave Goodbye" from the recording *Rumble to the Bottom* by Colleen and Uncle Squaty (Colleen and Uncle Squaty, 1997).

Have everyone in the audience follow the motions in the song. My lyrics were originally intended as a lively good-bye rap and became the text for the toddler book *Wave Goodbye*, published by Lee and Low. Brian Schellinger, of the musical duo Colleen and Uncle Squaty, wrote a laid-back melody to my words, which makes for a mellow ending to this particular program theme.

> Wave high, wave low,
> I think it's time, we gotta go.
> Wave your elbows, wave your toes,
> Wave your tongue and wave your nose.
> Wave your knees, wave your lips,
> Blow a kiss with fingertips.
> Wave your ears, wave your hair,
> Wave your belly and derriere.
> Wave your chin, wave your eye,
> Wave your hand and say "Goodbye!"

SCHOOL TALENT SHOW

Program at a Glance

Opening Song: "Four Boys Named Jordan" by Jessica Harper
Hello Song: "Hello" by Dan Zanes
Picture Book: *Horace and Morris Join the Chorus (but What about Dolores?)* by James Howe
Song: "You'll Sing a Song and I'll Sing a Song" by Ella Jenkins

Picture Book: *The Music Teacher from the Black Lagoon* by Mike Thaler
Song: "That's What I Learned in School"
Picture Book: *Miss Bindergarten Plans a Circus with Kindergarten* by Joseph Slate
Song: "There's a Dog in School" by Bill Wellington
Picture Book: *Four Boys Named Jordan* by Jessica Harper
Picture Book: *Matthew A.B.C.* by Peter Catalanotto
Song: "Z Y X" by They Might Be Giants
Good-bye Song: "Blow a Kiss" by Laurie Berkner

Preparation and Presentation

Opening Song

"Four Boys Named Jordan" from the recording *Inside Out* by Jessica Harper (Rounder, 2001).

Have the recording play as the audience enters the story program area. The lyrics feature a classroom that has four students, each named Jordan. The song shows up later in the program.

Hello Song

"Hello" from the recording *Rocket Ship Beach* by Dan Zanes (Festival Five, 2000).

Sing this pretty, simple tune (there are only three chords) or let Zanes and company do it for you. Say hello to the morning sky, friends, the sun, and clouds. Say hello in Hebrew, Spanish, Italian, French, Japanese, Arabic, Korean, Chinese, and Polish. The lyrics and chords can be found on Zanes's website: www.danzanes.com.

Picture Book

Horace and Morris Join the Chorus (but What about Dolores?) by James Howe, illustrated by Amy Walrod (Atheneum, 2002).

Horace, Morris, and Dolores all love to sing. Unfortunately, Dolores sings "notes no one had ever heard before." She's brokenhearted when the other two make the chorus, and she's encouraged to be in the audience. She writes a note to Moustro Provolone, the choir director. He recognizes her writing ability, puts music to her words, and invites her to sing in the chorus. This is one of the most enjoyable picture books to read aloud, especially the singing parts. Sing an off-key "The Mouse in the Wheel Goes Round and Round" with gusto.

Song

"You'll Sing a Song and I'll Sing a Song" from the recording *You'll Sing a Song and I'll Sing a Song* by Ella Jenkins (Smithsonian Folkways, 1989).

This is one of the prettiest original children's songs ever written, and it's very simple to sing. Tell the children that this will be a good song for Horace, Morris, and Dolores to sing in their chorus. Use Jenkins as a model as she works with children to sing together "in warm or wintry weather." Jenkins includes verses for playing a tune, humming, and whistling.

Picture Book

The Music Teacher from the Black Lagoon by Mike Thaler, illustrated by Jared Lee (Scholastic, 2000).

A boy is worried about his new music teacher. Reportedly, she wears armor, breaks children's glasses by hitting a high C, makes you memorize a zillion notes, and zaps you with her laser baton if you miss one note. Of course, he finds out that his music teacher is really cool.

Song

"That's What I Learned in School." Traditional.

This song has been known for generations under a variety of titles such as "My Hand on My Head," "Tinkerboxer," and "Wiggle the Wool." Body parts are given new nonsensical names. Each line ends with "that's what I learned in school." Have the children rub the featured body part during this cumulative song.

> 1. With my hand on my head,
>   What have I here?
>   This is my top-notcher,
>   My teacher dear.
>   Top-notcher, top-notcher,
>   Wiggle the wool,
>   That's what I learned in my school.
>
> 2. With my hand on my eyes,
>   What have I here?
>   These are my eye-blinkers,
>   My teacher dear.
>   Eye-blinkers . . . top-notcher,
>   Wiggle the wool.
>   That's what I learned in my school.
>
> 3. With my hand on my nose,
>   What have I here?
>   This is my smell-sniffer,
>   My teacher dear.

Smell-sniffer . . . eye-blinkers . . . top-notcher,
Wiggle the wool,
That's what I learned in my school.

4. mustache . . . soup-strainer . . .
5. mouth . . . food-chomper . . .
6. chin . . . chin-chopper . . .

Some versions continue with other body parts. The song "My Hand on My Head," found on the recording *Wee Sing Silly Songs* by Pamela Beall and Susan Nipp (Price Stern Sloan, 1982), includes "brow . . . sweat-boxer," "chest . . . air-blower," "stomach . . . bread basket," "lap . . . lap-sitter," "knee . . . knee-bender," and "foot . . . foot-stomper." "My Hand on My Head" can also be found on the recording *Dr. Jean and Friends* (Jean Feldman, 1998).

The version "Tinkerboxer" can be found on the recording *Friends, Forever Friends* by the Parachute Express (Trio Lane, 1996).

The version "Wiggle the Wool" can be found on the recording *Fingerplays, Movement and Story Songs* by Colleen and Uncle Squaty (Colleen and Uncle Squaty, 1993).

Picture Book

Miss Bindergarten Plans a Circus with Kindergarten by Joseph Slate, illustrated by Ashley Wolff (Dutton, 2002).

The children in Miss Bindergarten's class create props and costumes for a school circus presentation. They also work on publicity, set up the chairs, learn tricks, and make food. The star attraction turns out to be Miss Bindergarten herself when she appears as the mysterious Jugglebee.

Song

"There's a Dog in School" from the recording *Radio WOOF Goes Back to School* by Bill Wellington (Well-in-Tune, 2005).

This simple, hilarious pattern song is one of those songs that makes everyone say, "Why didn't I think of that?" Wellington wrote the lyrics about a dog who attends school. Since the dog is in school, everyone has to "woof" the alphabet. Later, everyone clucks and snorts the alphabet when a chicken and a pig join the school. The song can also be found on the following recordings:

Stotts, Stuart, and Tom Pease. *Celebrate: A Song Resource*. Tomorrow River, 2000.

Peterson, Carole. *H.U.M.—All Year Long*. Macaroni Soup, 2003.

Picture Book

Matthew A.B.C. by Peter Catalanotto (Atheneum, 2002).

This is my all-time favorite alphabet book. A teacher has twenty-five boys, all named Matthew. Matthew A is extremely affectionate and clings to his teacher throughout the book. Matthew F has a cat on his face. Matthew Y yodels. And so on. At the end of the book, the teacher gets a new student—Matthew Z. His clothing is full of zippers.

Song

"Z Y X" from the recording *Here Come the ABCs* by They Might Be Giants (Disney, 2005).

Follow up the zany alphabet book with one of the many songs that features a backward alphabet. Hold up a chart that lists the letters of the alphabet in reverse order. Listen to the rock group They Might Be Giants as they sing the alphabet backward in a slow, "serious" tone.

Other songs that feature singing or reciting the alphabet in reverse order include

"ABCs." Ralph's World. *Ralph's World*. Mini Fresh, 2001.

"The Alphabet Boogie." Fink, Cathy. *When the Rain Came Down*. Rounder, 1988.

"The Alphabet Song." Beall, Pamela, and Susan Nipp. *Wee Sing in the Car*. Price Stern Sloan, 1999.

"The Funky Backwards Alphabet." Mr. Al. *Rockin' the Alphabet*. Cradle Rock, 1998.

Picture Book

Four Boys Named Jordan by Jessica Harper, illustrated by Tara Calahan King (Putnam, 2004).

Start to wind up the program with the picture-book version of the song the audience heard as they entered the room. Elizabeth, the narrator, complains when a fourth boy named Jordan joins the classroom. Roll call is a mess when the teacher "asks if Jordan's present." If you ask Jordan for some scissors, "you'll end up with four pairs." Things get worse when the class gets a new girl. Her name? Jordan!

Good-bye Song

"Blow a Kiss" from the recording *Under a Shady Tree* by Laurie Berkner (Two Tomatoes, 2002).

Play the recording for no other reason than to make kissing noises to get a reaction from the kids. The lyrics to this good-bye song can be found on Berkner's website: www.twotomatoes.com.

TOOT! TOOT! BEEP! BEEP! STORIES AND SONGS ABOUT TRAVEL AND VEHICLES
Program at a Glance

Opening Song: "Take a Ride" by Rebecca Frezza
Hello Song: "Howdy Song" by Monty Harper
Picture Book: *How Will You Get There, Maisy?* by Lucy Cousins
Song: "Me, Myself and I" by Kimmy Schwimmy
Picture Book: *The Wheels on the School Bus* by Mary-Alice Moore
Picture Book: *Here Comes Grandma!* by Janet Lord
Song: "She'll Be Comin' 'round the Mountain," adapted by Dana
Picture Book: *I'm Dirty!* by Kate McMullan
Song: "Drivin' in My Car" by Ralph's World
Good-bye Song: "Goodbye" by Yosi

Preparation and Presentation

Opening Song

"Take a Ride" from the recording *Tall and Small* by Rebecca Frezza (Big Truck, 2006).

As audience members enter the story program area, play this lively transportation song. The lyrics can be found on Frezza's website: www.bigtruckmusic .com.

Hello Song

"Howdy Song" from the recording *Take Me to Your Library* by Monty Harper (Monty Harper, 2003).

Play Harper's recording and let the children sing the response part of each verse.

> 1. In Oklahoma, we say "Howdy!" (Howdy!) (2x)
>   So when you meet your friend on the street,
>   You'll say "Howdy" if you're thinking on your feet.
>   It's a mighty fine way to share your day with a fellow human being.
>
> 2. In Mexico, they say "Hola!" (Hola!) (2x)
>   So when you meet your "amigo" on the street,
>   You'll say "Hola" if you're thinking on your feet.
>   It's a mighty fine way to share your day with a fellow human being.

3. In Germany, they say "Guten Tag." (Guten Tag) (2x)
   So when you meet your "freund" on the street,
   You'll say "Guten Tag" if you're thinking on your feet.
   It's a mighty fine way to share your day with a fellow human being.

4. In Japan, they say "Konnichiwa." (Konnichiwa) (2x)
   So when you meet your "tomodachi" on the street,
   You'll say "Konnichiwa" if you're thinking on your feet.
   It's a mighty fine way to share your day with a fellow human being.

5. In Russia, they say "Privet." (Privet) (2x)
   So when you meet your "droog" on the street,
   You'll say "Privet" if you're thinking on your feet.
   It's a mighty fine way to share your day with a fellow human being.

6. In the USA, we say all of these and more,
   'cause people living here came here from every single shore.
   Doesn't matter how you say "How do you do."
   It's a happy little holler, makes the world a little smaller.
   It's a message you send to connect to a friend.
   It's a mighty fine way to share your day with a fellow human being.
   Howdy, y'all!

Picture Book

How Will You Get There, Maisy? by Lucy Cousins (Candlewick, 2004).

This lift-the-flap format immediately engages the audience with questions about traveling. Will Charlie get to the farm with apples, horseshoes, and a saddle on a motorcycle? A picture shows Charlie standing next to a motorcycle, which is wrong. Lift the flap to reveal the right answer—a horse. This pattern continues with a hot air balloon/rocket, tractor/train, sled/plane, car/boat, skateboard/fire engine, and bus/bike.

Song

"Me, Myself and I" from the recording *Kimmy Schwimmy Music*, vol. 1, by Kimmy Schwimmy (North Corner, 2005).

This is a fun movement and sound-effects song. Kimmy has good directions on her website: www.kimmyschwimmy.com. Visit her site and download her songbook.

1. Me, Myself and I are going for a ride on a train
   Ch ch ch ch ch ch ch ch woo woo!

Going for a ride on a train
Ch ch ch ch ch ch ch ch woo woo!
I'm going for a ride, just Me, Myself and I.

2. Me, Myself and I are going for a ride on a plane
Mreeeaar mreeeaar
Going for a ride on a plane
Mreeeaar mreeeaar
I'm going on a ride, just Me, Myself and I.

3. Me, Myself and I are going for a ride in a car
Beep beep beep, beep beep beep
Going for a ride in a car
Beep beep beep, beep beep beep
I'm going for a ride, just Me, Myself and I.

4. Me, Myself and I are going for a ride on a horse
Neigh-brr neigh-brr neigh
Going for a ride on a horse
Neigh-brr neigh-brr neigh
I'm going for a ride, just Me, Myself and I.
I'm going for a ride, just Me, Myself and I.
Beep bop bip bop bibbity dow.

Picture Book

The Wheels on the School Bus by Mary-Alice Moore, illustrated by Laura Huliska-Beith (HarperCollins, 2006).

The kids on the school bus say, "Off to school"; the teachers on the bus say, "Think, think, think"; the coach says, "Catch, catch, catch"; the nurse says, "Open wide"; the lunch ladies say, "Eat, eat, eat"; and—my favorite—the librarian on the bus says, "Read, read, read." The bus driver turns out to be the principal. Sing the lyrics, and the kids will join you. If you're not familiar with the tune, ask the kids. They'll know it.

Picture Book

Here Comes Grandma! by Janet Lord, illustrated by Julie Paschkis (Holt, 2005).

Grandma is coming to see you in a variety of ways. She'll pull on her boots "and walk a long way to see you." She'll ride a bicycle, leap on a horse, drive a car, hop on a train, slip on snow skis, sail a hot-air balloon, swim underwater, ride in a plane, and give you a big hug when she sees you. Kids will notice Grandma is joined on her journey by a dog.

Song

"She'll Be Comin' 'round the Mountain" from the recording *Dana's Best Travelin' Tunes* by Dana (RMFK, 1995).

The picture book *Here Comes Grandma!* is a perfect match for the traditional song "She'll Be Comin' 'round the Mountain," which can be found on scores of children's recordings. Dana has added new verses to make the song even sillier.

1. She'll be comin' 'round the mountain when she comes (toot toot). (2x)
   She'll be comin' 'round the mountain, she'll be comin' 'round the mountain,
   She'll be comin' 'round the mountain when she comes (toot toot).

2. She'll be driving six white horses when she comes (yeehaw)
   . . . She'll be driving them crazy when she comes (yeehaw, toot toot).

3. We'll all run out to meet her when she comes (Howdy Ma'am)
   . . . And we'll all be glad to meet her when she comes (Howdy Ma'am, yeehaw, toot toot).

4. And she'll smother us with kisses when she comes (ooh yuk!)
   We'll be covered with lipstick when she's done (ooh yuk, Howdy Ma'am, yeehaw, toot toot).

5. She'll be wearin' too much perfume when she comes (pee-yew)
   . . . We won't be able to breathe until she's gone (pee-yew, ooh yuk, Howdy Ma'am, yeehaw, toot toot).

6. She'll bring way too much luggage when she comes (lug lug)
   . . . And we'll all have to lug it when she comes (lug lug, pee-yew, ooh yuk, Howdy Ma'am, yeehaw, toot toot).

7. But we'll still be glad to see her when she comes (oh yeah!)
   . . . 'Cause she loves us and we love her, yes we do (oh yeah, lug lug, pee-yew, ooh yuk, Howdy Ma'am, yeehaw, toot toot).

Picture Book

I'm Dirty! by Kate McMullan, illustrated by Jim McMullan (HarperCollins, 2006).

I'm a big fan of the McMullans' book *I Stink!* featuring an anthropomorphic garbage truck, as well as their book *I'm Mighty!* which features a tugboat. Any of these titles will work well with this theme. Since kids are crazy about construction equipment, and this particular title features a busy backhoe loader who cleans up a junkyard, this book gets the nod. The text is a treat to read aloud. "Who's got a boom, a dipper stick, and a bucket with a row of chompers?" The illustrations are also fun to look at as the backhoe cleans up "broken bicycles," "scuffed-up signs," and "tossed-out toilet seats" before taking a mud bath.

Song

"Drivin' in My Car" from the recording *Ralph's World* by Ralph's World (Mini Fresh, 2001).

Ralph sings a very, very simple ditty about driving to Minneapolis. On subsequent verses, he substitutes the song's words for sound effects, such as car horn ("beep beep beep beep"), windshield wipers ("swish swish swish swish"), car muffler (a series of "raspberry" noises with your tongue), and waving to a friend you see on the street ("hi hi hi hi"). This song is loads of fun.

Good-bye Song

"Goodbye" from the recording *Monkey Business* by Yosi (Yosi, 2002).

You can sing this song, or let Yosi sing this farewell to everyone around the world. Encourage the kids to say each word for *good-bye* along with the words in quotation marks.

I can say "adios" in Spanish, Spanish, Spanish,
Let's say "adios" in Spanish,
"Adios" means goodbye.
I can say "ciao" in Italian, Italian, Italian,
Let's say "ciao" in Italian,
"Ciao" means goodbye.

Chorus:
So, now smile. Shake someone's hand.
Say goodbye in their language,
In another land.

Let's say "do svidanja" in Russian, Russian, Russian,
Let's say "do svidanja" in Russian,
"Do svidanja" means goodbye.
Let's say "sayonara" in Japanese, Japanese, Japanese,
Let's say "sayonara" in Japanese,
"Sayonara" means goodbye.

(Chorus)

"Adios" means goodbye.
"Ciao" means goodbye.
"Do svidanja" means goodbye.
"Sayonara" means goodbye.
And the French say "au revoir,"
Which means 'til we meet again.

Fun Pairings
Matching Children's Songs with Picture Books

While listening to the *thousands* of songs for the companion book, *Children's Jukebox*, second edition, it became routine for me to automatically think, "I know a good picture book to pair with that song." Some of those pairings went into the story program themes section of this book. Other odds-and-ends pairings are listed below. I would particularly like to spotlight the musical recording *Literacy in Motion* by the Learning Station for developing songs around specific children's books and musician Elizabeth McMahon for her excellent ability to craft new songs around traditional folk tales.

Song	Book
"Ain't We Crazy" from *A Child's Celebration of Silliest Songs* (Music for Little People, 1999)	*Bright and Early Thursday Evening* by Audrey Wood (Harcourt, 1996)
"Anansi" from *Corner Grocery Store* by Raffi (Troubadour, 1979)	*Anansi and the Moss-Covered Rock* by Eric Kimmel (Holiday House, 1988)
"Angry" from *Literacy in Motion* by the Learning Station (Monopoli/Learning Station, 2005)	*When Sophie Gets Angry—Really, Really Angry* by Molly Bang (Scholastic, 1999)
"Ants in My Pants" from *Late Last Night* by Joe Scruggs (Educational Graphics, 1984)	*Got to Dance* by M. C. Helldorfer (Doubleday, 2003)

"The Awful Hilly Daddy-Willie Trip" from *Mail Myself to You* by John McCutcheon (Rounder, 1988)

Night Driving by John Coy (Holt, 1996)

"Awfullish Day" from *Just a Little Hug* by Hans Mayer (Windwall, 1996)

Alexander and the Terrible, Horrible, No Good, Very Bad Day by Judith Viorst (Atheneum, 1972)

"Baba Yaga" from *I Sang It Just for You* by Mary Kaye (Mary Kaye, 2003)

Baba Yaga by Eric Kimmel (Holiday House, 1991)

"Billy Goats Gruff" from *Magic Parade* by Elizabeth McMahon (Mrs. McPuppet, 2006)

The Three Billy Goats Gruff by Paul Galdone (Clarion, 1973)

"Blue Jay" from *Blue Jay, Blue Jay!* by Paul Strausman (A Gentle Wind, 1997)

Brown Bear, Brown Bear, What Do You See? by Bill Martin Jr. (Holt, 1967)

"Bobo and Fred" from *Rock 'n' Roll Teddy Bear* by Rosenshontz (Lightyear, 1992)

"Freddie" from *Kids Pick the Funniest Poems* by Bruce Lansky (Meadowbrook, 1991)

"Boiled Okra and Spinach" from *Mine!* by Trout Fishing in America (Trout, 1994)

Princess Picky by Marjorie Priceman (Roaring Brook, 2002)

"A Brontosaurus with Bronchitis" from *Naughty Songs for Boys and Girls* by Barry Louis Polisar (Rainbow Morning, 1993)

How Do Dinosaurs Get Well Soon? by Jane Yolen (Scholastic, 2003)

"Brown Bear, Brown Bear, What Do You See?" from *Playing Favorites* by Greg and Steve (Youngheart, 1991)

Brown Bear, Brown Bear, What Do You See? by Bill Martin Jr. (Holt, 1967)

"Casey Jones" from *My Mama Was a Train* by James Coffey (Blue Vision 2002)

Casey Jones by Allan Drummond (Frances Foster, 2000)

"Change the Baby" from *Ants* by Joe Scruggs (Educational Graphics, 1994)

Amelia Bedelia and the Baby by Peggy Parish (Greenwillow, 1981)

"Chicken Soup with Rice" from *Cookin'* by Gary Rosen (GMR, 1996)

Chicken Soup with Rice: A Book of Months by Maurice Sendak (HarperCollins, 1962)

"Climb That Beanstalk" from *The Classroom Boogie* by Tom Knight (Tom Knight, 2003)

Jack and the Beanstalk by Steven Kellogg (Morrow, 1991)

"Country Mouse and City Mouse" from *Magic Parade* by Elizabeth McMahon (Mrs. McPuppet, 2006)

Town Mouse, Country Mouse by Jan Brett (Putnam, 1994)

"Cousins" from *Mother Earth* by Tom Chapin (Sundance, 1990)

The Relatives Came by Cynthia Rylant (Bradbury, 1985)

"Cow in the Car" from *Dana's Best Travelin' Tunes* by Dana (RMFK, 1995)

Sakes Alive! A Cattle Drive by Karma Wilson (Little, Brown, 2005)

"The Cricket Song" from *The Frog's Party* by Mary Lu Walker (A Gentle Wind, 1989)

The Very Quiet Cricket by Eric Carle (Philomel, 1990)

"Dinosaurs and the Progress of Man" from *Foote Prints* by Norman Foote (Disney, 1991)

We're Back: A Dinosaur's Story by Hudson Talbott (Crown, 1987)

"Dirt Made My Lunch" from *Dirt Made My Lunch* by the Banana Slug String Band (Music for Little People, 1987)

We Love the Dirt by Tony Johnston (Scholastic, 1997)

"Don't Be Rude to a Rhinoceros" from *I've Got a Yo-Yo* by Tom Paxton (Rounder, 1997)

Who Wants a Cheap Rhinoceros? by Shel Silverstein (Macmillan, 1964)

"Down on the Funny Farm" from *Uh-Oh!* by Rosenshontz (Lightyear, 1991)

The Cow Who Clucked by Denise Fleming (Holt, 2006)

"Eat, Repeat" from *What's Eatin' Yosi?* by Yosi (Yosi, 2006)

Penelope and the Humongous Burp by Sheri Radford (Lobster, 2004)

"Eensy Weensy Spider" from *Deep in the Jungle* by Joe Scruggs (Educational Graphics, 1987)

Diary of a Spider by Doreen Cronin (Joanna Cotler, 2005)

"A Fairy Went A-Marketing" from *Daydreamer* by Priscilla Herdman (Music for Little People, 1993)

A Fairy Went A-Marketing by Rose Pyleman (Dutton, 1986)

"Father Grumble" from *Howjadoo* by John McCutcheon (Rounder, 1986)

The Man Who Kept House by P. C. Asbjornsen and J. E. Moe (Margaret K. McElderry, 1992)

"Follow the Drinking Gourd" from *Shakin' a Tailfeather* (Music for Little People, 1997)

Follow the Drinking Gourd by Jeanette Winter (Knopf, 1988)

"The Garden" from *Unbearable Bears* by Kevin Roth (Marlboro, 1985)

Frog and Toad Together by Arnold Lobel (HarperCollins, 1971)

"Genie Fish" from *Sci-Fi Hi-Fi* by Ken Lonnquist (Kenland, 1999)

The Fisherman and His Wife by Rosemary Wells (Dial, 1998)

"Get Your Own Goat" from *Little Ears: Songs for Reading Readiness* by Fran Avni (Leapfrog School House, 2000)

Gregory the Terrible Eater by Mitchell Sharmat (Scholastic, 1980)

"The Gingerbread Man" from *Dana's Best Rock and Roll Fairy Tales* by Dana (RMFK, 1999)

The Gingerbread Man by Jim Aylesworth (Scholastic, 1998)

"The Giving Song" from *Literacy in Motion* by the Learning Station (Monopoli/Learning Station, 2005)

The Giving Tree by Shel Silverstein (HarperCollins, 1964)

"Going through the Car Wash" from *Popcorn and Other Songs to Munch On* by Rick Charette (Pine Point, 1994)

Car Wash by Sandra Steen (Putnam, 2001)

"Goldilocks Rap" from *Teddy Bear's Greatest Hits* by Bill Shontz (Bearspaw, 1997)

Goldilocks and the Three Bears by James Marshall (Dial, 1988)

"Good Night Moon" from *Feel the Music* by the Parachute Express (Disney, 1991)

Goodnight Moon by Margaret Wise Brown (HarperCollins, 1947)

"Great Machine" from *Sing It! Say It! Stamp It! Sway It!* vol. 3, by Peter and Ellen Allard (80-Z Music, 2002)

Construction Countdown by K. C. Olson (Holt, 2004)

"Green Eggs and Ham" from *Literacy in Motion* by the Learning Station (Monopoli/Learning Station, 2005)

Green Eggs and Ham by Dr. Seuss (Random House, 1960)

"Hard Scrabble Harvest" from *Daydreamer* by Priscilla Herdman (Music for Little People, 1993)

Hard Scrabble Harvest by Dahlov Ipcar (Doubleday, 1976)

"Head to Toe Dance" from *Literacy in Motion* by the Learning Station (Monopoli/Learning Station, 2005)

Head to Toe by Eric Carle (HarperCollins, 1997)

"A House Is a House for Me" from *Rhyme a Word or Two* by Fred Penner (Casablanca Kids, 2004)

A House Is a House for Me by Mary Ann Hoberman (Viking, 1978)

"How I Became a Clown" from *Some Assembly Required* by Tom Chapin (Razor & Tie, 2005)

Olivia Saves the Circus by Ian Falconer (Atheneum, 2001)

"Hundredth Day of School" from *Monkey Business* by Stephen Fite (Melody House, 1998)

100th Day Worries by Margery Cuyler (Simon & Schuster, 2000)

"Hungry Caterpillar" from *Literacy in Motion* by the Learning Station (Monopoli/Learning Station, 2005)

The Very Hungry Caterpillar by Eric Carle (Philomel, 1969)

"I Don't Wanna Go to School" from *Teacher's Favorites* by Barry Louis Polisar (Rainbow Morning, 1993)

First Day Jitters by Julie Danneberg (Charlesbridge, 2000)

"I Got a Wiggle" from *1, 2, 3, Four-Ever Friends* by Colleen and Uncle Squaty (Colleen and Uncle Squaty, 1995)

Wiggle by Doreen Cronin (Atheneum, 2005)

"I Had an Old Coat" from *Good Kid* by Peter and Ellen Allard (Peter and Ellen Allard, 2000)

Joseph Had a Little Overcoat by Simms Taback (Viking, 1999)

"I Love Mud" from *Alligator in the Elevator* by Rick Charette (Pine Point, 1985)

Mud Puddle by Robert Munsch (Annick, 1982)

"I M 4 U" from *Scat like That* by Cathy Fink and Marcy Marxer (Rounder, 2005)

CDB! by William Steig (Simon & Schuster, 1968)

"I Wonder If I'm Growing" from *Singable Songs for the Very Young* by Raffi (Troubadour, 1976)

Happy Birthday, Sam by Pat Hutchins (Greenwillow, 1978)

"I Wouldn't Be Scared, Not Me" from *One Big Dance* by Stuart Stotts (Tomorrow River, 1996)

Nathaniel Willy, Scared Silly by Judith Matthews and Fay Robinson (Bradbury, 1994)

"If I Ran the World" from *Family Garden* by John McCutcheon (Rounder, 1993)

Title poem from *If I Were in Charge of the World* by Judith Viorst (Atheneum, 1981)

"It's Better Than That" from *InFINity* by Trout Fishing in America (Trout Records, 2001)

The Secret Knowledge of Grown-ups by David Wisniewski (HarperCollins, 1998)

"It's OK" from *Tickles You!* by Rosenshontz (Lightyear, 1991)

Two Terrible Frights by Jim Aylesworth (Atheneum, 1987)

"John Henry" from *Howjadoo* by John McCutcheon (Rounder, 1986)

John Henry by Julius Lester (Dial, 1994)

"Juicy Black Fly" from *Blast Off!* by Ben Rudnick (Ben Rudnick, 2004)

Old Black Fly by Jim Aylesworth (Holt, 1995)

"King Midas" from *I Sang It Just for You* by Mary Kaye (Mary Kaye, 2003)

King Midas: The Golden Touch by Demi (Margaret K. McElderry, 2001)

"Kiss the Baby Goodnight" from *Sing It! Say It! Stamp It! Sway It!* vol. 3, by Peter and Ellen Allard (80-Z Music, 2002)

I Kissed the Baby by Mary Murphy (Candlewick, 2003)

"Lazy Mary, Will You Get Up?" from *Morning Magic* by Joanie Bartels (BMG, 1987)

"Lazy Jane" from *Where the Sidewalk Ends* by Shel Silverstein (HarperCollins, 1974)

"The Little Engine That Could" from *Burl Ives Sings Little White Duck* by Burl Ives (Columbia, 1974)

The Little Engine That Could by Watty Piper (Platt and Munk, 1954)

"The Little Red Hen" from *Blue Sky Sparklin' Day* by Elizabeth McMahon (Rosie Rhubarb, 1993)

The Little Red Hen by Jerry Pinkney (Dial, 2006)

"A Little Red Jeep" from *Toad Motel* by Rick Charette (Pine Point, 1999)

Sheep in a Jeep by Nancy Shaw (Houghton Mifflin, 1986)

"Me-tronome" from *Good Kid* by Peter and Ellen Allard (Peter and Ellen Allard, 2000)

Max Found Two Sticks by Brian Pinkney (Simon & Schuster, 1994)

"The Mitten" from *Blue Sky Sparklin' Day* by Elizabeth McMahon (Rosie Rhubarb, 1993)

The Mitten by Jan Brett (Putnam, 1989)

"Mixing Colors" from *Tot Rock* by Gary Rosen (Lightyear, 1993)

Mouse Paint by Ellen Stoll Walsh (Harcourt, 1989)

"Mud" from *Summersongs* by John McCutcheon (Rounder, 1995)

Mud Puddle by Robert Munsch (Annick, 1982)

"Mushroom Umbrellas" from *The Frog's Party* by Mary Lu Walker (A Gentle Wind, 1989)

Mushroom in the Rain by Mirra Ginsburg (Macmillan, 1974)

"My Dad" from *Where Do My Sneakers Go at Night?* by Rick Charette (Pine Point, 1987)

Day Out with Daddy by Stephen Cook (Walker, 2006)

"My Favorite Kind of Bug" from *Giddyup!* by Buck Howdy (Prairie Dog Entertainment, 2005)

Insects Are My Life by Megan McDonald (Orchard, 1995)

"My Old Jalopy" from *Who's Got a Hug?* by the Parachute Express (Trio Lane, 1998)

Rattletrap Car by Phyllis Root (Candlewick, 2001)

"My Trip down the Drain" from *Where Do My Sneakers Go at Night?* by Rick Charette (Pine Point, 1987)

The Tub People by Pam Conrad (HarperCollins, 1989)

"The Night the Froggies Flew" from *Fingerplays, Movement and Story Songs* by Colleen and Uncle Squaty (Colleen and Uncle Squaty, 1993)

Tuesday by David Wiesner (Clarion, 1991)

"No No No No" from *Literacy in Motion* by the Learning Station (Monopoli/Learning Station, 2005)

No, David by David Shannon (Scholastic, 1998)

"Off to Bed" from *Look at My Belly* by Brady Rymer (Bumblin' Bee, 2002)

Goodnight Moon by Margaret Wise Brown (HarperCollins, 1947)

"On the Day You Were Born" from *Hello World* by Red Grammer (Red Note, 1995)

On the Day You Were Born by Debra Frasier (Harcourt, 1991)

"One Crane" from *Wobbi-Do-Wop* by Tom Pease (Tomorrow River, 1993)

Sadako by Eleanor Coerr (Putnam, 1993)

"Owl Moon" from *Daddy Starts to Dance* by Tom Pease (Tomorrow River, 1996)

Owl Moon by Jane Yolen (Philomel, 1987)

"Pecos Bill" from *Giddyup!* by Buck Howdy (Prairie Dog Entertainment, 2005)

Pecos Bill by Steven Kellogg (Morrow, 1986)

"Pig Latin Polka Dance" from *Scat like That* by Cathy Fink and Marcy Marxer (Rounder, 2005)

Giggle, Giggle, Quack by Doreen Cronin (Simon & Schuster, 2002)

"Princess and the Pea" from *The Lost Songs of Kenland* by Ken Lonnquist (Kenland, 1998)

The Princess and the Pea in Miniature by Lauren Child (Hyperion, 2006)

"Rapunzel Got a Mohawk" from *Ants* by Joe Scruggs (Educational Graphics, 1994)

Rapunzel: A Happenin' Rap by David Vozar (Doubleday, 1998)

"Red Brontosaurus" from *Kimmy Schwimmy Music*, vol. 1, by Kimmy Schwimmy (North Corner, 2005)

Brown Bear, Brown Bear, What Do You See? by Bill Martin Jr. (Holt, 1967)

"Sad, Bad, Terrible Day" from *Literacy in Motion* by the Learning Station (Monopoli/Learning Station, 2005)

Alexander and the Terrible, Horrible, No Good, Very Bad Day by Judith Viorst (Atheneum, 1972)

"Sally Eats Shoelaces, Straw and String" from *Old Enough to Know Better* by Barry Louis Polisar (Rainbow Morning, 2005)

Gregory the Terrible Eater by Mitchell Sharmat (Scholastic, 1980)

"Six in the Bed" from *Here We Go Loopty Loo* by the Learning Station (Monopoli/Learning Station, 1998)

Bed Hogs by Kelly DiPucchio (Hyperion, 2004)

"Spider and the Fly" from *Sci-Fi Hi-Fi* by Ken Lonnquist (Kenland, 1999)

The Spider and the Fly by Mary Botham Howitt and Tony DiTerlizzi (Simon & Schuster, 2002)

"Stinky Cake" from *Stinky Cake* by Carole Peterson (Macaroni Soup, 2005)

I Stink! by Kate and Jim McMullan (HarperCollins, 2002)

"Stone Soup" from *Make Believe* by Linda Arnold (Ariel, 1986)

Stone Soup by Jon Muth (Scholastic, 2003)

"There's a Bowl of Milk in the Moonlight" sung by Gunnar Madsen on *Hear and Gone in 60 Seconds* (Rounder, 2003)

Kitten's First Full Moon by Kevin Henkes (Greenwillow, 2004)

"There's a Werewolf under My Bed" from *On the Trail* by Troubadour (A Gentle Wind, 1990)

I Was a Second Grade Werewolf by Daniel Pinkwater (Dutton, 1983)

"The Three Little Pigs Blues" from *Playing Favorites* by Greg and Steve (Youngheart, 1991)

The Three Little Pigs by Steven Kellogg (Morrow, 1997)

"Tiny Mosquito" from *Old Mr. Mackle Hackle* by Gunnar Madsen (G-Spot, 1999)

Zzzng! Zzzng! Zzzng! A Yoruba Tale by Phillis Gershator (Orchard, 1998)

"Twins" from *Nobody Else like Me* by Cathy Fink and Marcy Marxer

Hello Twins by Charlotte Voake (Candlewick, 2006)

"Underwear" from *Teacher's Favorites* by Barry Louis Polisar (Rainbow Morning, 1993)

Underwear Do's and Don'ts by Todd Parr (Little, Brown, 2000)

"Walkin' on My Wheels" from *A Friend, a Laugh, a Walk in the Woods* by Dan Crow (Allshouse, 2000)

Zoom! by Robert Munsch (Scholastic, 2003)

"Who's Afraid of the Big Bad Wolf?" from *The Day I Read a Book* by Bill Shontz (Bearspaw, 1998)

Beware of the Storybook Wolves by Lauren Child (Scholastic, 2001)

"Why Did I Have to Have a Sister?" from *10 Carrot Diamond* by Charlotte Diamond (Hug Bug, 1985)

Angelina's Baby Sister by Katherine Holabird (C. N. Potter, 1991)

"Wild Things" from *Literacy in Motion* by the Learning Station (Monopoli/ Learning Station, 2005)

Where the Wild Things Are by Maurice Sendak (HarperCollins, 1963)

"Yertle the Turtle" from *A Child's Celebration of Song 2* (Music for Little People, 1996)

Yertle the Turtle by Dr. Seuss (Random House, 1958)

"The Yodel Polka" from *Grandma Slid down the Mountain* by Cathy Fink (Rounder, 1987)

Sing, Sophie! by Dayle Ann Dodds (Candlewick, 1997)

More Musical Ideas

Here is an odds-and-ends listing of musical programming ideas that might come in handy. They are listed in alphabetical order by song title. Each entry contains the recording artist and recording(s) on which the song can be found. This listing is just the tip of the iceberg of wonderful musical ideas that can be found in children's musical recordings. Explore the various recordings, and discover the many great ideas out there.

"Abazaba Scooby Dooby." Arnold, Linda. *Happiness Cake*. Ariel, 1988.

Children love to learn new phrases (remember "supercalifragilisticexpiali-docious"?). Teach them the words the girl in the song says whenever she gets into trouble: "Abazaba scooby dooby apa choka maka yeah."

"ABC Nursery Rhyme Game." Beall, Pamela, and Susan Nipp. *Wee Sing in the Car*. Price Stern Sloan, 1999.

Sing the alphabet to the tune of "99 Bottles" and then sing a nursery rhyme afterward to the same tune. You'll be amazed at how simple it is.

"All You Et-A." Beall, Pamela, and Susan Nipp. *Wee Sing in the Car*. Price Stern Sloan, 1999.

This simple traditional cumulative song is sung to the tune of "Alouette." You can solicit different food items from the audience.

"The Ants Go Marching." Colleen and Uncle Squaty. *Rumble to the Bottom*. Colleen and Uncle Squaty, 1997.

Make ant stick puppets by fastening black felt circles on Popsicle sticks. Have the children march around the room with the puppets while listening to the recording.

"Baby Bird." Beall, Pamela, and Susan Nipp. *Wee Sing Children's Songs and Fingerplays.* Price Stern Sloan, 1977.

There's plenty of movement in this short, simple traditional song. Young children can act out a baby bird leaving its egg and learning to fly only to fall down, down, down.

"Bathtub Blues." Brown, Greg. *Bathtub Blues.* Red House, 1993.

The singer gets so dirty that he has to take a bath every night. He eventually turns into a duck. Play the recording and let the audience chime in on the call-and-response lines.

"Bathtub Soup." Rymer, Brady. *I Found It!* Bumblin' Bee, 2004.

Fill a baby plastic tub with a rubber duckie, sponges, boats, letters, bubbles, washcloths, and plastic sea creatures as you listen to the recording. Stir this "soup" with a large spoon.

"Beanbag Boogie." Greg and Steve. *Kids in Motion.* Youngheart, 1987.

Play the recording, and balance beanbags on body parts as the singers instruct. Try it with tissue for younger kids (or less agile adults in the audience).

"The Bear Hunt." The Learning Station. *Here We Go Loopty Loo.* Monopoli/Learning Station, 1998.

Here is one of the few musical versions of this extremely popular storytime movement activity.

"The Bear That Snores." Roth, Kevin. *Unbearable Bears.* Marlboro, 1985.

The noise that keeps a bear awake is the bear itself snoring. Kids will be able to snore away during the chorus while you play the recording.

"Bellybutton." Pease, Tom. *I'm Gonna Reach!* Tomorrow River, 1989.

Any song that encourages audience members to sing the word *bellybutton* dozens of times along with the recording has to be good.

"Bingo." Greg and Steve. *We All Live Together*, vol. 4. Youngheart, 1980.

Greg and Steve sing the traditional song "Bingo" but bark in place of clapping. "B-I-bark-bark-bark . . ."

"Black Socks." Harley, Bill. *Monsters in the Bathroom.* Round River, 1984.

This traditional camp favorite explains why black socks never need washing. It is fairly easy for older kids to learn as a straight rendition or as a round.

"Boa Constrictor." Peter, Paul, and Mary. *Peter, Paul, and Mommy.* Warner Brothers, 1969.

Paint a large snake on a bed sheet, and slowly pull it up in front of you while singing this simple Shel Silverstein composition. A sleeping bag works, too.

"Bodies 1-2-3." Allard, Peter and Ellen. *Sing It! Say It! Stamp It! Sway It!* vol. 2. 80-Z Music, 1999.

This extremely simple song encourages kids to wiggle fingers, bend knees, swing arms, blink eyes, and more . . . "'til they stop."

"Can You Sound Just like Me?" Grammer, Red. *Can You Sound Just like Me?* Smilin' Atcha, 1983.

Follow Grammer's vocal gymnastics in this simple sound-effects/call-and-response tune.

"Candy Man, Salty Dog." Sharon, Lois, and Bram. *Great Big Hits.* Elephant, 1992.

Play the recording and follow along with singer Bram in this simple and infectious call-and-response song.

"The Children of the World Say Hello." Barchas, Sarah. *Bridges across the World.* High Haven, 1999.

There are several songs that feature greetings in foreign languages. A few other select titles include

> "Hello." Arnold, Linda. *Peppermint Wings.* Ariel, 1990.
>
> "Hello." Gemini. *The Best of Gemini.* Gemini, 1998.
>
> "Hello to the Children of the World." Beall, Pamela, and Susan Nipp. *Wee Sing around the World.* Price Stern Sloan, 1994.
>
> "Many Ways to Say Hello." Silberg, "Miss Jackie." *Joining Hands with Other Lands.* Kimbo, 1993.
>
> "'Round the World with Ways to Say Hello." Palmer, Hap. *Can a Jumbo Jet Say the Alphabet?* Hap-Pal, 1998.
>
> "Siyanibingelela." Grunsky, Jack. *Jack in the Box 1.* Casablanca Kids, 2001.
>
> "Way over There." Colleen and Uncle Squaty. *1, 2, 3, Four-Ever Friends.* Colleen and Uncle Squaty, 1995.

"Clean-O." Guthrie, Woody. *Woody Guthrie's 20 Grow Big Songs.* Warner Brothers, 1992.

Children can act out scrubbing their faces, ears, hair, knees, and feet while listening to the recording.

"Cluck, Cluck, Red Hen." Raffi. *Corner Grocery Store.* Troubadour, 1979.

Sing this simple song that goes to the tune of "Baa, Baa, Black Sheep." Hold up pictures of a sheep, hen, cow, and bee with a "cheat sheet"—the lyrics written on the back of each picture.

"Comin' down the Chimney." The Learning Station. *Seasonal Songs in Motion.* Monopoli/Learning Station, 2001.

This is a fun Christmas version of the popular activity song "She'll Be Comin' 'round the Mountain."

"The Cool Bear Hunt." Feldman, Jean. *Dr. Jean Sings Silly Songs.* Jean Feldman, n.d.

This musical version of "Bear Hunt" finds Dr. Jean leading her audience through a candy factory, a peanut-butter river, and a Jello swamp.

"Do Your Ears Hang Low?" Sharon, Lois, and Bram. *Great Big Hits 2.* Elephant, 2002.

I've gotten more mileage from performing this trio's version of this song with tights on my head (see the photo in my book *Family Storytime*, ALA Editions, 1999). New verses include movements for eyes, nose, and mouth.

"Doggie." Grammer, Red. *Can You Sound Just like Me?* Smilin' Atcha, 1983.

Kids can make sniffing, licking, snoring, and howling noises. Try singing the song without the recording. The tune is simple, and the words are easy to learn.

"Dogs." Crow, Dan. *Oops!* Rounder, 1988.

Play the recording of this hilarious dog song. There are several opportunities for the kids to go "woof" and "arf" as they listen.

"Donald Duck." Allard, Peter and Ellen. *Sing It! Say It! Stamp It! Sway It!* vol. 2. 80-Z Music, 1999.

The quacks at the end of each line of this very simple tune will elicit lots of giggles.

"Down on the Farm." Greg and Steve. *We All Live Together,* vol. 5. Youngheart, 1994.

Kids make rooster, cow, pig, dog, horse, turkey, donkey, and people noises to the tune of "The Wheels on the Bus." Extremely simple.

"Down the Sidewalk" Big Jeff. *Big Jeff.* Big Jeff, 2000.

Turn into different animals while waiting for the light to change. Kids move like the animal and make the appropriate sound.

"The Eensy Weensy Spider." Sharon, Lois, and Bram. *Mainly Mother Goose.* Elephant, 1984.

In addition to singing about the "eensy weensy" spider, this trio sings about the "BIG FAT" spider, with overly large motions, as well as the "teensy weensy" spider, with miniscule motions.

"18 Wheels on a Big Rig." Trout Fishing in America. *Family Music Party.* Trout, 1998.

This is one of the funniest original children's songs ever recorded. Play it and enjoy. Here's a small list of what I feel are the funniest original children's songs on the market:

> "Barbie's Head Is Missing." Harley, Bill. *I Wanna Play.* Round River, 2007.
>
> "Don't Make Me Sing Along." Simmons, Al. *The Celery Stalks at Midnight.* Casablanca Kids, 1996.
>
> "The Elephant Who Couldn't Pay Rent." Pullara, Steve. *One Potato, Two Potato.* Cool Beans, 1995.
>
> "I Never See Maggie Alone." Ralph's World. *Peggy's Pie Parlor.* Mini Fresh, 2003.
>
> "If You Have a Kid Who Complains All the Time." Polisar, Barry Louis. *Old Enough to Know Better.* Rainbow Morning, 2005.
>
> "I've Got a Dog and My Dog's Name Is Cat." Polisar, Barry Louis. *Family Concert.* Rainbow Morning, 1993.
>
> "The Zucchini Song." Crow, Dan. *A Friend, a Laugh, a Walk in the Woods.* Allshouse, 2000.

"Everyone Counts." Moo, Anna. *Anna Moo Crackers.* Moosic, 1994.

Count one, two, three in Spanish, German, and Japanese and then count again in dog (woof, woof, woof), rooster, pig, and dolphin.

"Everybody Eats When They Come to My House." Sharon, Lois, and Bram. *Great Big Hits 2.* Elephant, 2002.

Listen to the recording as the singers match food items with names, such as *salami* with *Tommy, gravy* with *Davey, banana* with *Hannah,* and more. See what rhyming combinations the kids in your audience can make. One of my kids rhymed Rob with shish kebab.

"Everybody Has a Face." Peterson, Carole. *Tiny Tunes.* Macaroni Soup, 2005.

Sing to the tune of "Old MacDonald" and blink eyes "with a blink, blink here and a blink, blink there." Other verses include actions and sound effects for noses, mouths, and cheeks.

"The Freeze." Greg and Steve. *Kids in Motion.* **Youngheart, 1987.**

Play the recording to this, one of many movement songs that instruct the audience to move around and then freeze in place. Other "freeze-type" songs include

"Follow the Directions." SteveSongs. *Little Superman.* SteveSongs, 2003.

"The Freeze Game." Beall, Pamela, and Susan Nipp. *Wee Sing Games, Games, Games.* Price Stern Sloan, 1986.

"Silly Dance Contest." Gill, Jim. *Jim Gill Sings the Sneezing Song and Other Contagious Tunes.* Jim Gill, 1993.

"Stop and Go." LaFond, Lois. *Turning It Upside Down.* Rockadile, 1994.

"Wiggy Wiggles Freeze Dance." Palmer, Hap. *Two Little Sounds.* Hap-Pal, 2003.

"Goin' to the Coral Reef." Arnold, Linda. *Splash Zone.* **Youngheart, 2000.**

This is a fun visit to a coral reef similar to the style of the popular movement activity "Going on a Bear Hunt."

"Goin' to the Zoo." Paxton, Tom. *Goin' to the Zoo.* **Rounder, 1997.**

This modern-day classic is the best children's zoo song on the market. Play the recording and let the kids sing "Goin' to the zoo, zoo, zoo."

"Grandpa's Farm." Fink, Cathy, and Marcy Marxer. *A Cathy & Marcy Collection for Kids.* **Rounder, 1994.**

Instruct the kids to suggest a farm animal, what color it is, and then the sound it makes. Fit new verses right into the song's simple pattern. For extra fun, add nonfarm animals and inanimate objects.

"Grandpa's Truck." Ode, Eric. *Grandpa's Truck.* **Deep Rooted, 2003.**

This fun sound-effects song works well by dividing the audience into four groups and assigning the different truck noises to each group.

"The Growing Song." Atkinson, Lisa. *I Wanna Tickle the Fish.* **A Gentle Wind, 1987.**

The second half of the song turns into a round to the tune of "Row, Row, Row Your Boat." The kids slowly stand as they sing "children get taller" and slowly kneel when they sing "grown-ups get smaller."

"Happy Birthday." Chapin, Tom. *Great Big Fun for the Very Little One.* **Sundance, 2001.**

This is not the traditional birthday song but one set to the music of Franz Lehár's "The Merry Widow Waltz."

"Head, Shoulders, Knees, and Toes." Bartels, Joanie. *Bathtime Magic.* BMG, 1990.

Bartel's version of this traditional song directs the children to make washing motions on their heads, shoulders, knees, toes, eyes, ears, mouths, and noses.

"Hey Lolly Lolly." Beall, Pamela, and Susan Nipp. *Wee Sing Sing-Alongs.* Price Stern Sloan, 1982.

This simple traditional song is fun rhyming kids' names with activities. For example, "I know a boy named Mike. Hey lolly, lolly-o. He likes to ride a bike. Hey lolly, lolly-o." Some names are challenging to rhyme, but use your imagination. For example, match Jessica with wearing a vest-ica. (Be prepared for groans to follow.)

"How Much Is That Doggie in the Window?" Sharon, Lois, and Bram. *Great Big Hits.* Elephant, 1992.

Sharon, Lois, and Bram's version of this song has also become a staple in my workshops. Divide the audience into three parts. One group sings "Bull! Dog!" the second group sings "Chihuahua," and the last group sings "Terrier." The leader sings the title song over this background cacophony.

"I Like to Read." Mayer, Hans. *See You Later, Alligator.* Myther, 1997.

Sing the phrases ("I like to read books and magazines") in a style similar to the popular wordplay song "Apples and Bananas."

"I See a Horsie." Silberg, "Miss Jackie." *Peanut Butter, Tarzan, and Roosters.* Miss Jackie, 1981.

Start with animal names and noises for this pattern song. "I see a cow, what does it say? Moo!" Move on to children's names. "I see an Ali, what does she say? Hee-hee!" Model Silberg's interaction with the children on the recording.

"I Wish I Was." Rosenshontz. *Tickles You!* Lightyear, 1991.

Have kids name an animal and think of an action that rhymes with that animal, such as "I wish I was a mouse. I'd sleep inside your house." Rosenshontz includes rhymes for dogs, gorillas, ostriches, monkeys, bears, and camels. See what they do with hippopotamus.

"If Animals Could Dance." The Learning Station. *La Di Da La Di Di Dance with Me.* Monopoli/Learning Station, 2004.

This simple yet imaginative song lets kids decide how different animals dance.

"If I Could Be Anything." Pelham, Ruth. *Under One Sky*. A Gentle Wind, 1982.

> Pelham sings that she would be happy to be with you even if she was a raindrop, a pair of argyle socks, or a garden shovel. Add your own verses to this pretty call-and-response song.

"If You Love a Hippopotamus." Kaldor, Connie. *A Duck in New York City*. Folle Avoine, 2003.

> Lead the children in a hippo walk while playing the recording. Don't know how a hippo walks? Ask a kid and follow whatever directions he or she gives.

"I'm a Three-Toed, Triple-Eyed, Double-Jointed Dinosaur." Polisar, Barry Louis. *Old Dog, New Tricks*. Rainbow Morning, 1993.

> This is the best dinosaur song on the market. Play the recording and watch how quickly the kids learn the tongue-twisting chorus.

"I'm a Tree." Banana Slug String Band. *Dirt Made My Lunch*. Music for Little People, 1987.

> A deep "tree" voice sings this simple cumulative song that is full of sounds the children can make, such as the wind, birds, and squirrels.

"I'm in the Mood." Raffi. *Rise and Shine*. Troubadour, 1982.

> Raffi is in the mood for singing, clapping, whistling, and stomping. This simple song is ready-made for children to add their own verses, such as humming or dancing.

"I'm So Mad I Could Scream." Silberg, "Miss Jackie." *Peanut Butter, Tarzan, and Roosters*. Miss Jackie, 1981.

> Cover your ears as the kids make the noises associated with the emotions portrayed in the song: mad enough to scream and stomp, sad enough to cry, and glad enough to sigh.

"It's Time to Go to Bed." Charette, Rick. *Chickens on Vacation*. Pine Point, 1990.

> Charette sings out, "It's time to go to bed," to which the audience can respond in whining voices, "Do I have to go to bed?" The recording has a fun twist when the adults in the song get tired and the kids tell them, "It's time to go to bed!"

"Join in the Game." Greg and Steve. *Playing Favorites*. Youngheart, 1991.

> Everyone will be up and clapping, giggling, snoring, hiccupping, and sneezing to this simple song. Add your own verses.

"The Journey Dance." Pirtle, Sarah. *Magical Earth*. A Gentle Wind, 1993.

Pirtle acts as a caller leading the children to dance as if they were moving through peanut butter, applesauce, and marshmallows. She also directs children to turn in a circle, slide, and make a pretzel shape before bowing to their partners and resting their "weary bones."

"Jump." Avni, Fran. *Artichokes and Brussel Sprouts*. Music for Little People, 1988.

Kids are instructed to jump, stamp, or walk tiptoe while placing their hands in several positions in this offbeat follow-the-directions song. Avni has basically created a dance version of the popular game Twister.

"Jump Children." Marxer, Marcy. *Jump Children*. Rounder, 1997.

Marxer asks the children if they want to jump. The kids respond with a loud "Yeah" and proceed to jump. She asks if they want to dance with the same results. Add your own suggestions.

"Just Not Fair." Nagler, Eric. *Improvise with Eric Nagler*. Rounder, 1989.

Nagler sings about the injustices kids suffer at the hands of adults: bathing more than once a year, wearing clean underwear, and so on. Play the recording and let the kids shout "It's just not fair!" at the appropriate times.

"The Kitchen Percussion Song." The Chenille Sisters. *1-2-3 for Kids*. Red House, 1990.

Break out the kitchen utensils and let the children play them as instruments. There are places in the recording to bang spoons, pots, pans, and whatever you can round up.

"Late at Night When I'm Hungry." Charette, Rick. *Bubble Gum*. Educational Activities, 1983.

This highly participative song has the kids sneaking around at night. It closes with everyone saying good night to the stars, the moon, the fish, their toes, and their stomachs.

"Late Last Night." Scruggs, Joe. *Late Last Night*. Educational Graphics, 1984.

Play the recording and let the audience act out the movements to wearing ballet shoes, space boots, roller skates, cleats, and more.

"Little Red Wagon." Buchman, Rachel. *Hello, Everybody*. A Gentle Wind, 1986.

Buchman gives very specific movement directions in her variation of this traditional song. The children will be crawling, wagging their fingers, jumping, walking, jolting, and falling down.

"Looby Loo." Sharon, Lois, and Bram. *One Elephant, Deux Éléphants.* **Elephant, 1980.**

Many folks don't realize this traditional song is thought to be about taking a hot bath on a Saturday night. "You put your right hand in" to check if the water is too hot. This is an easy, fun movement song to sing and act out.

"Many Cows." Pease, Tom. *Boogie! Boogie! Boogie!* **Tomorrow River, 1986.**

The kids can echo the recording as Pease sings "many, many, many, many, many, many cows." It wouldn't be a good cow song if there weren't also ample chances for the kids to sing "Moo!"

"A Mind of His Own." Parachute Express. *Friends, Forever Friends.* **Trio Lane, 1996.**

Kids can learn and sing the chorus with the kids on the recording: "Dittily, Umpa-Dittily, Ha-Ha-Ha." They will laugh as the brother in the song creates new words for things, such as "licky sticks" for lollipops and "twinkle dots" for stars. Ask the kids to invent new words for everyday objects.

"Must Be Working." Kinder, Brian. *A Kid like You.* **Brian Kinder, 2002.**

This is probably my favorite goofy movement song of all time. Play the recording and let Kinder direct your motions.

"My Bonnie." Gill, Jim. *Jim Gill Sings Do Re Mi on His Toe Leg Knee.* **Jim Gill, 1999.**

Gill revives an old camp song. Sing the traditional song "My Bonnie Lies over the Ocean" and raise your hands every time you sing a word that starts with the letter *B*. Gill adds other fun movements.

"My Dog Rags." Cassidy, Nancy. *Nancy Cassidy's KidsSongs.* **Klutz Press, 2004.**

Teach the children to move their hands by their ears as Rags "goes flip-flop." Have them wiggle their hips when Rags "goes wig-wag," and finally, point in different directions when Rags "goes zig-zag."

"My Roots Go Down." Pirtle, Sarah. *Two Hands Hold the Earth.* **A Gentle Wind, 1984.**

Pirtle sings about being a pine tree, a willow, a wildflower, and a waterfall. Each verse is repeated three times to invite the whole group to sing along.

"Name Game." Ralph's World. *Ralph's World.* **Mini Fresh, 2001.**

This is the easiest (and possibly goofiest) name song on the market. Pick a name and sing it over and over and over.

"Old MacDonald Had a Band." Raffi. *Singable Songs for the Very Young.* **Troubadour, 1976.**

Raffi's version includes banjo, guitar, jug, fiddle, and singers instead of animals. Kids can imitate the sounds with their mouths and act out playing the instruments.

"Old MacDonald Had a 'Whzz.'" Silberg, "Miss Jackie." *Peanut Butter, Tarzan, and Roosters.* Miss Jackie, 1981.

On this Old MacDonald spin-off, "Miss Jackie" uses mouth sounds such as tongue clicks, lip burbles, raspberries, coughs, and sneezes. Very, very simple.

"On a Cold and Frosty Morning." Buchman, Rachel. *Sing a Song of Seasons.* Rounder, 1997.

Make three simple felt crows with a circle for the head and triangles for the body, tail, and beak. Remove the felt crows one by one as you sing this very simple folk song.

"The Other Side of the World." Pirtle, Sarah. *Magical Earth.* A Gentle Wind, 1993.

Point to the various countries on a globe or world map as Pirtle sings about Braulio in Santiago, Li-min in Canton, Miriam in Jerusalem, Kuraluk in the Arctic, Ahmed in Cairo, Chipo in Sweden, and several other children around the world.

"The People in the Car." Scruggs, Joe. *Traffic Jams.* Educational Graphics, 1985.

This song features outrageous sound effects. There are noises for the radio, horn, blinkers, radiator, brakes, tires, muffler, transmission, and more. In the end, the people in the car get out and push.

"Polly the Parrot." Grunsky, Jack. *Jack in the Box 2.* Casablanca Kids, 2001.

Who better to lead a call-and-response song than a parrot? Polly leads the audience through reciting musical instruments, taking a bath, and throwing an animal party. Use a parrot puppet if you have one (although the song is still fun if you don't).

"Puddles." Diamond, Charlotte. *My Bear Gruff.* Hug Bug, 1992.

This call-and-response song features boots that go smacking and tongues catching raindrops. Everyone hops like a frog while splashing in the puddles.

"Pussy Willow Riddle." Buchman, Rachel. *Hello Everybody.* A Gentle Wind, 1986.

This traditional song is all about the pussy that will never be a cat. Buchman instructs the children to sing with their whole bodies. She directs them to crouch and slowly grow (stand up) as the simple song progresses.

"Put Your Thumb in the Air." Scruggs, Joe. *Deep in the Jungle.* Educational Graphics, 1987.

Listen to Scruggs, and before you know it, everyone will be twisted like pretzels in one of my favorite movement songs.

"Riding in My Car." Guthrie, Woody. *Woody's 20 Grow Big Songs.* **Warner Brothers, 1992.**

There are plenty of sound effects in this simple car song. The children will find themselves click-clacking the door, rattling on the front seat, making a "brrm" engine noise, and blowing the horn with a loud "a-oorah, a-oougah."

"Rocky Shore Symphony." Arnold, Linda. *Splash Zone.* Youngheart, 2000.

Arnold encourages the kids to make seashore sound effects for waves, bubbles, the wind, crabs, clams, and penguins.

"Row Your Boat." Williams, Robin and Linda. *Down in the Valley.* A Gentle Wind, 1982.

This camp favorite finds the performers singing "Row Your Boat" several times but dropping the last word each time they sing it. Challenging but fun.

"Sarah the Whale." Sharon, Lois, and Bram. *Name Games.* Casablanca Kids, 2002.

Sing the song once and then repeat it, leaving out some words for the kids to fill in. This tune, sung to the melody of "Dixie," is a good memory exercise.

"School Shoes." Kinder, Brian. *A Kid like You.* Brian Kinder, 2002.

A kid forgets to wear his school shoes and instead wears his dancing shoes, hopping shoes, skipping shoes, and running shoes in this movement song.

"Shaker Song." Pelham, Ruth. *Under One Sky.* A Gentle Wind, 1982.

Pelham's simple musical directions describe how to put gravel into an egg carton to create a rhythm instrument. Do this as a craft activity and then play the instruments to the recording.

"She'll Be Comin' 'round the Mountain." Beall, Pamela, and Susan Nipp. *Wee Sing in the Car.* Price Stern Sloan, 1999.

This version has a hot rod ("brm brm"), rowboat ("splash splash"), airplane ("zoom zoom"), and taxi ("beep beep").

"Shoo Fly." Mitchell, Elizabeth. *You Are My Flower.* Last Affair, 1998.

Cut a felt circle for a fly and tie it to a string. Dangle the "fly" in front of a frog puppet. Pretend the puppet is singing the song. Have it "gulp" the fly at the end of the song, and watch the kids go into hysterics.

"Show Me What You Feel." Greg and Steve. *Kids in Motion.* Youngheart, 1987.

This upbeat song will let kids act out their emotions. They'll show how they feel when they're happy, mad, excited, hungry, and so on.

"Simon Says." Greg and Steve. *We All Live Together*, vol. 3. Youngheart, 1979.

Greg and Steve have created a musical version of the popular elimination game that is easier for young children and has no winners or losers.

"Skinnamarink." Sharon, Lois, and Bram. *Great Big Hits 2*. Elephant, 2002.

Sing this simple song, and have the audience point to their eyes when you sing "I," point to their hearts when "love" is sung, and point to someone else when you sing "you."

"Skip to My Lou." Greg and Steve. *We All Live Together*, vol. 1. Youngheart, 1975.

The inventive duo adds commands to the traditional song such as "touch your toes, skip to my lou," "flap your wings, skip to my lou," "bang your drum, skip to my lou," and more.

"Sleep, Sleep." Rosenshontz. *Share It*. Lightyear, 1982.

This is one of the best bedtime songs on the market. Play the recording and let the kids sing the refrain "Sleep, sleep, ya gotta go to sleep" over and over.

"Smile." Beall, Pamela, and Susan Nipp. *Wee Sing Sing-Alongs*. Price Stern Sloan, 1982.

This traditional song is sung to the tune of "The Battle Hymn of the Republic." "It isn't any trouble just to S-M-I-L-E." The formula is set for other verses, such as "L-A-U-G-H" and "G-R-I-N grin!" The last verse finds everyone singing "ha-ha-ha" throughout.

"Spider on the Floor." Raffi. *Singable Songs for the Very Young*. Troubadour, 1976.

Use a spider puppet and have it crawl up your leg, stomach, neck, face, and head while singing this very simple song. If you don't have a spider puppet, use your hand and fingers to simulate a spider.

"There's a Hippo in My Tub." Bartels, Joanie. *Bathtime Magic*. BMG, 1990.

The narrator knows that she should take a bath but tells Mom she can't because of the hippo, penguins, and crocodile in the tub. Play the recording while bouncing puppets of the above in a plastic infant tub.

"This Old Man." Dana. *Dana's Best Sing and Play-a-Long Tunes*. RMFK, 1995.

Dana's hip version of the traditional song has a catchy rap that the kids will quickly learn. "We got the knick, we got the knack, we got the knick, we got the knack, we got the paddy-whack!"

"The Trans Canadian Super Continental Special Express." Penner, Fred. *Fred's Favourites*. Casablanca Kids, 2004.

The kids will love singing the tongue-twisting title phrase over and over. There are also plenty of "whoo-whoo," "chugga-chugga," and other train sound effects.

"Travelin' Jack." Mr. Al. *Put Your Groove On*. Cradle Rock, 2002.

Jack meets a bear, lion, and snake and goes walking, running, bouncing, rolling, and swimming in this fun alternative to the traditional movement activity "We're Going on a Bear Hunt."

"A Walking We Will Go." Greg and Steve. *We All Live Together*, vol. 5. Youngheart, 1994.

This very simple song has the kids walking, stomping, skipping, sliding, bouncing, tip-toeing, and marching to the tune of "A-Hunting We Will Go."

"Watermelon." McCutcheon, John. *Family Garden*. Rounder, 1993.

Play the recording and act out eating a big slice of watermelon. The chorus is full of sound effects such as slurping, spitting "the seeds," and saying "ahhh."

"When I First Came to This Land." Diamond, Charlotte. *10 Carrot Diamond*. Hug Bug, 1985.

Make motions for the kids to perform while listening to the recording. For example, hold your back for "break my back," make milking motions and shake your head for "no milk now," and make a muscle for "muscle in my arm."

"Whole Bed." Scruggs, Joe. *Bahamas Pajamas*. Educational Graphics, 1990.

Scruggs sings the traditional song "Ten in the Bed" and ends by breaking into "I've got the whole mattress to myself" to the tune of "He's Got the Whole World."

"Wiggle in My Toe." Scruggs, Joe. *Late Last Night*. Educational Graphics, 1984.

The kids will find wiggles in their toes, feet, knees, seats, tummies, arms, hands, head, and hair in this cumulative song. Play the recording and wiggle away.

"Willoughby Wallaby Woo." Raffi. *Singable Songs for the Very Young*. Troubadour, 1976.

Follow Raffi's patterns of adding or substituting the letter *W* to the beginning of someone's name. Thus, Sam becomes "Wam" and Julia becomes "Wulia."

"You Can't Make a Turtle Come Out." Ungar, Jay, and Lyn Hardy. *A Place to Be.* A Gentle Wind, 1981.

Sing this wonderful Malvina Reynolds song while holding a turtle puppet that has a retractable head. Use your hand and thumb as a less-expensive alternative.

"You Gotta Sing." Raffi. *More Singable Songs.* Troubadour, 1977.

You gotta sing, dance, shout, wiggle, and shake when the spirit moves you. Add your own verses to this very simple, traditional pattern song.

Call-and-Response Songs

Call-and-response songs are usually easy, program-friendly songs. Simply play the recordings and follow the performers' cues to sing specific words or phrases back. The following songs may appear on more than one recording although only one source is listed here. Check with the companion book, *Children's Jukebox*, second edition, for a complete listing of sources for each song.

"ABC Rock." Greg and Steve. *We All Love Together*, vol. 1. Youngheart, 1975.

"ABCs." Mayer, Hans. *Stars of the Swing Set*. Myther, 1999.

"Adjectives and Nouns." Crow, Dan. *The Word Factory*. Allshouse, 2000.

"Aerobics." Fink, Cathy, and Marcy Marxer. *Bon Appétit!* Rounder, 2003.

"Akwa Nwa Nere Nnwa." Beall, Pamela, and Susan Nipp. *Wee Sing around the World*. Price Stern Sloan, 1994.

"All Hid." Sharon, Lois, and Bram. *School Days*. Casablanca Kids, 2004.

"The Alligator Chant." Feldman, Jean. *Dr. Jean Sings Silly Songs*. Jean Feldman, n.d.

"Alouette." Penner, Fred. *Sing with Fred*. Casablanca Kids, 2002.

"Alphabet Rag." Harper, Monty. *Imagine That*. Monty Harper, 1996.

"Always Room for One More." Stotts, Stuart, and Tom Pease. *Celebrate: A Song Resource*. Tomorrow River, 2000.

"Are We There Yet?" Big Jeff. *Big Jeff*. Big Jeff, 2000.

"Barnyard Blues." Ralph's World. *Happy Lemon*. Mini Fresh, 2001.

"Bathtub Blues." Brown, Greg. *Bathtub Blues*. Red House, 1993.

"The Bear." Beall, Pamela, and Susan Nipp. *Wee Sing Fun 'n' Folk*. Price Stern Sloan, 1989.

"The Bear Went over the Mountain." Greg and Steve. *Ready, Set, Move!* Greg and Steve, 2004.

"The Beat." LaFond, Lois. *I Am Who I Am*. Zoom Express, 1985.

"Beat of My Heart." Grunsky, Jack. *Jack in the Box 2*. Casablanca Kids, 2001.

"Bento Uri." Raven, Nancy. *Jambalaya!* Lizard's Rock, 2003.

"Big, Bigger, Biggest." Jenkins, Ella. *Growing Up with Ella Jenkins*. Smithsonian Folkways, 2002.

"Bill Grogan's Goat." Beall, Pamela, and Susan Nipp. *Wee Sing Animals, Animals, Animals*. Price Stern Sloan, 1999.

"Blues in B♭." LaFond, Lois. *Turning It Upside Down*. Rockadile, 1994.

"Boo Boo Bunny." Rosen, Gary. *Tot Rock*. Lightyear, 1993.

"Boo Hoo." LaFond, Lois. *I Am Who I Am*. Zoom Express, 1985.

"Buono Appetito." Grammer, Red. *Hello World*. Red Note, 1995.

"Butterfly." Atkinson, Lisa. *The Elephant in Aisle Four*. A Gentle Wind, 2000.

"Bye-Bye Pizza Pie." Parachute Express. *Sunny Side Up*. Disney, 1991.

"Cadima." Jenkins, Ella. *You'll Sing a Song and I'll Sing a Song*. Smithsonian Folkways, 1989.

"Can Cockatoos Count by Twos?" Palmer, Hap. *Can Cockatoos Count by Twos?* Hap-Pal, 1996.

"Can You Sound Just like Me?" Grammer, Red. *Can You Sound Just like Me?* Smilin' Atcha, 1983.

"Candy Man, Salty Dog." Sharon, Lois, and Bram. *Everybody Sing!* Casablanca Kids, 2002.

"Captain T." Kinder, Brian. *One More Time*. Brian Kinder, 2004.

"Che Che Kule." Colleen and Uncle Squaty. *Movin' Party*. Colleen and Uncle Squaty, 2001.

"The Children of the World Say Hello." Barchas, Sarah. *Bridges across the World*. High Haven, 1999.

"Chopping the Cane." Raven, Nancy. *Jambalaya!* Lizard's Rock, 2003.

"Cinco de Mayo." Barchas, Sarah. *¡Piñata! and More*. High Haven, 1997.

"Conejito en mi hombro." Alsop, Peter. *Uh-Oh!* Moose School, 2002.

"The Cool Bear Hunt." Feldman, Jean. *Dr. Jean Sings Silly Songs*. Jean Feldman, n.d.

"Cowboy Song." Kinder, Brian. *One More Time*. Brian Kinder, 2004.

"The Days of the Week." Diamond, Charlotte. *Diamond in the Rough*. Hug Bug, 1986.

"Did You Feed My Cow?" Various Artists. *cELLAbration! A Tribute to Ella Jenkins*. Smithsonian Folkways, 2004.

"Don't Think about Food." Kinder, Brian. *A Kid like You*. Brian Kinder, 2004.

"Don't You Just Know It." Harley, Bill. *There's a Pea on My Plate*. Rounder River, 1997.

"Down by the Bay." Barchas, Sarah. *If I Had a Pony*. High Haven, 1996.

"Down by the Ocean." Allard, Peter and Ellen. *Sing It! Say It! Stamp It! Sway It!* vol. 2. 80-Z Music, 1999.

"Down the Do-Re-Mi." Grammer, Red. *Down the Do-Re-Mi*. Red Note, 1991.

"Dulce Dulce." Jenkins, Ella. *You'll Sing a Song and I'll Sing a Song*. Smithsonian Folkways, 1989.

"Echo." Harley, Bill. *Down in the Backpack*. Rounder River, 2001.

"Echo Gecko." Kinder, Brian. *A Kid like You*. Brian Kinder, 2002.

"Eh-un-lan-weh-she-un-lan (Greeting in Arabic)." Jenkins, Ella. *Multicultural Children's Songs*. Smithsonian Folkways, 1995.

"Elephants Have Wrinkles." Colleen and Uncle Squaty. *Sing-a-Move-a-Dance*. Colleen and Uncle Squaty, 2005.

"Flea Fly." Allard, Peter and Ellen. *Sing It! Say It! Stamp It! Sway It!* vol. 2. 80-Z Music, 1999.

"The Frog Song." Harper, Monty. *The Great Green Squishy Mean Concert CD*. Monty Harper, 2005.

"Fruits and Vegetables." Barchas, Sarah. *Get Ready, Get Set, Sing!* High Haven, 1994.

"Fun-a-Rooey." Kinnoin, Dave. *Fun-a-Rooey*. Song Wizard, 1987.

"Funga Alafia." Barchas, Sarah. *Bridges across the World*. High Haven, 1999.

"Funky Backwards Alphabet." Mr. Al. *Rockin' the Alphabet*. Cradle Rock, 1998.

"Getting Our Exercise." Kinder, Brian. *One More Time*. Brian Kinder, 2004.

"Goin' to the Coral Reef." Arnold, Linda. *Splash Zone*. Youngheart, 2000.

"Good Morning Sunshine." Grunsky, Jack. *Follow the Leader*. Casablanca Kids, 2002.

"Goodbye, My Friend." Pirtle, Sarah. *The Wind Is Telling Secrets*. A Gentle Wind, 1988.

"Good-bye, So Long, Farewell, Toodle-oo." Palmer, Hap. *Two Little Sounds*. Hap-Pal, 2003.

"Goodnight." Palmer, Hap. *Witch's Brew*. Educational Activities, 1978.

"Got to Be Good to Your Self." LaFond, Lois. *Lois LaFond and the Rockadiles*. Rockadile, 1998.

"Great Big Man." Peterson, Carole. *Stinky Cake*. Macaroni Soup, 2005.

"The Great Green Squishy Mean Bibliovore." Harper, Monty. *The Great Green Squishy Mean Concert CD*. Monty Harper, 2005.

"The Green Grass Grew All Around." Rosenthal, Phil. *The Green Grass Grew All Around*. American Melody, 1995.

"Greetings." Green Chili Jam Band. *Coconut Moon*. Squeaky Wheel, 1997.

"Grillo Julian." Raven, Nancy. *Nancy Raven Sings Her Favorites*. Lizard's Rock, 2003.

"Grins." Green Chili Jam Band. *Starfishing*. Green Chili Jam, 1993.

"Hand Jive." Greg and Steve. *We All Live Together*, vol. 4. Youngheart, 1980.

"Handyman." Mr. Al and Stephen Fite. *Back to School Again*. Melody House, 1996.

"Hello." Arnold, Linda. *Peppermint Wings*. Ariel, 1990.

"Hello, How Are You." Feldman, Jean. *Dr. Jean Sings Silly Songs*. Jean Feldman, n.d.

"Hello World." Grammer, Red. *Hello World*. Red Note, 1995.

"Hey Caterpillar." Avni, Fran. *I'm All Ears: Sing into Reading*. Starfish, 1999.

"Hi Dee Ho." Cosgrove, Jim. *Pick Me! Pick Me!* Hiccup, 2003.

"The Hi Dee Ho Man." Gill, Jim. *Jim Gill Sings the Sneezing Song and Other Contagious Tunes*. Jim Gill, 1993.

"I Am a Bubble." Diamond, Charlotte. *Charlotte Diamond's World*. Hug Bug, 2000.

"I Am a Pizza." Alsop, Peter. *Wha' D'Ya Wanna Do?* Moose School, 1983.

"I Believe Myself." Fink, Cathy, and Marcy Marxer. *Help Yourself*. Rounder, 1990.

"I Feel Good." Mr. Al. *Rockin' the Alphabet*. Cradle Rock, 1998.

"I Got a Mosquito." The Learning Station. *Seasonal Songs in Motion*. Monopoli/Learning Station, 2001.

"I Got My Axe." Simmons, Al. *Something Fishy at Camp Wiganishie*. Casablanca Kids, 1995.

"I Know a Chicken." Berkner, Laurie. *Whaddaya Think of That?* Two Tomatoes, 2000.

"I Like Potatoes." Greg and Steve. *We All Live Together,* vol. 5. Youngheart, 1994.

"I Was Glad." Tucker, Nancy. *Glad That You Asked.* A Gentle Wind, 1988.

"If You Feel It." The Learning Station. *Seasonal Songs in Motion.* Monopoli/Learning Station, 2001.

"I'm a Sea Star." Arnold, Linda. *Splash Zone.* Youngheart, 2000.

"I'm Changing." Jenkins, Ella. *Growing Up with Ella Jenkins.* Smithsonian Folkways, 2002.

"I'm Going to Leave Old Texas Now." Riders in the Sky. *Saddle Pals.* Rounder, 1987.

"I'm on My Way." Various Artists. *I'm Gonna Let It Shine.* Round River, 1991.

"I'm Playing with a Monster." Avni, Fran. *I'm All Ears: Sing into Reading.* Starfish, 1999.

"It's a Lovely Day." McMahon, Elizabeth. *Magic Parade.* Mrs. McPuppet, 2006.

"It's a Pizza." Fite, Stephen. *Cool to Be in School.* Melody House, 2004.

"It's Gonna Take Us All." Kinder, Brian. *A Kid like You.* Brian Kinder, 2002.

"Jambo." Various artists. *cELLAbration! A Tribute to Ella Jenkins.* Smithsonian Folkways, 2004.

"John the Rabbit." Mitchell, Elizabeth. *You Are My Flower.* Last Affair, 1998.

"Joining Hands with Other Lands." Silberg, "Miss Jackie." *Joining Hands with Other Lands.* Kimbo, 1993.

"The Jolly Bus Line." Jenkins, Ella. *This-a-Way, That-a-Way.* Smithsonian Folkways, 1989.

"Juba." Raven, Nancy. *You Gotta Juba.* Lizard's Rock, 2003.

"Jump Children." Marxer, Marcy. *Jump Children.* Rounder, 1987.

"Keep a Little Light." Gemini. *The Best of Gemini,* vol. 2. Gemini, 2005.

"Keep on Dancing." Avni, Fran. *Artichokes and Brussel Sprouts.* Music for Little People, 1988.

"Kitchen Sing Sing." Raffi. *Raffi Radio.* Troubadour, 1995.

"Kitty Kitty." Kinder, Brian. *Again.* Brian Kinder, 2003.

"Kwanzaa." The Learning Station. *Literacy in Motion.* Monopoli/Learning Station, 2005.

"Let's Alphabecise." Fite, Stephen. *Monkey Business.* Melody House, 1998.

"Let's Get Started." Mr. Al. *Mr. Al Concert Live.* Cradle Rock, 2004.

"Let's Go to the Market." Greg and Steve. *We All Live Together*, vol. 5. Youngheart, 1994.

"Let's Make Music." Dana. *Dana's Best Sing and Play-a-Long Tunes*. RMFK, 1995.

"Let's Read and Rock." Greg and Steve. *Ready, Set, Move!* Youngheart, 2004.

"Liesl Echo." Ralph's World. *Green Gorilla, Monster, and Me*. Disney, 2006.

"Life Is." Rosenshontz. *Tickles You!* Lightyear, 1991.

"Little Bitty Frog." Lonnquist, Ken. *Earthy Songs*. Kenland, 2006.

"Little Kid." Alsop, Peter. *Uh-Oh!* Moose School, 2002.

"Little Sir Echo." Sharon, Lois, and Bram. *Great Big Hits*. Elephant, 1992.

"The Littlest Worm." Byers, Kathy. *'Round the Campfire*. KT Music, 2004.

"Lonesome Valley." Seeger, Pete. *Pete Seeger's Family Concert*. Sony, 1992.

"Long John." Raven, Nancy. *You Gotta Juba*. Lizard's Rock, 2003.

"Lunch." Gemini. *The Best of Gemini*. Gemini, 1998.

"Many Pretty Trees All around the World." Jenkins, Ella. *Songs Children Love to Sing*. Smithsonian Folkways, 1996.

"Many Ways to Say Hello." Silberg, "Miss Jackie." *Joining Hands with Other Lands*. Kimbo, 1993.

"Martin Luther King." Fink, Cathy. *When the Rain Comes Down*. Rounder, 1988.

"Mind Your Manners." Mr. Al. *Put Your Groove On*. Cradle Rock, 2002.

"Miss Mary Mack." Jenkins, Ella. *You'll Sing a Song and I'll Sing a Song*. Smithsonian Folkways, 1989.

"Momma Makes Cookies." Kinder, Brian. *Again*. Brian Kinder, 2003.

"Monster Day." Arnold, Linda. *Peppermint Wings*. Ariel, 1990.

"Mr. Owl." Kimmy Schwimmy. *Kimmy Schwimmy Music*, vol. 1. North Corner, 2005.

"Must Be Working." Kinder, Brian. *A Kid like You*. Brian Kinder, 2002.

"My Aunt Came Back." Beall, Pamela, and Susan Nipp. *Wee Sing in the Car*. Price Stern Sloan, 1999.

"My Grandma's Cat." Pirtle, Sarah. *Magical Earth*. A Gentle Wind, 1993.

"My Teddy Bear." Kinder, Brian. *Again*. Brian Kinder, 2003.

"The Number Rock." Greg and Steve. *We All Live Together*, vol. 2. Youngheart, 1978.

"On My Birthday." Stotts, Stuart, and Tom Pease. *Celebrate: A Song Resource*. Tomorrow River, 2000.

"On Top of Spaghetti." Yosi. *What's Eatin' Yosi?* Yosi, 2006.

"The One and Only Me." Atkinson, Lisa. *The One and Only Me.* A Gentle Wind, 1989.

"One World." LaFond, Lois. *One World.* Rockadile, 1989.

"Opposites." Greg and Steve. *Fun and Games.* Youngheart, 2002.

"The Other Day." The Learning Station. *Here We Go Loopty Loo.* Monopoli/Learning Station, 1998.

"Part of the Family." LaFond, Lois. *One World.* Rockadile, 1989.

"Pat Your Daddy." Alsop, Peter. *Uh-Oh!* Moose School, 2002.

"Percussive Vowels." Kimmy Schwimmy. *Kimmy Schwimmy Music,* vol. 1. North Corner, 2005.

"Poco." Penner, Fred. *Sing with Fred.* Casablanca Kids, 2002.

"Peanut Butter and Jelly." Greg and Steve. *Fun and Games.* Youngheart, 2002.

"Please." Barchas, Sarah. *Bridges across the World.* High Haven, 1999.

"Polly the Parrot." Grunsky, Jack. *Jack in the Box 2.* Casablanca Kids, 2001.

"Puddles." Diamond, Charlotte. *My Bear Gruff.* Hug Bug, 1992.

"Rabbit on My Shoulder." Alsop, Peter. *Uh-Oh!* Moose School, 2002.

"Rain Rain." Silberg, "Miss Jackie." *Sing about Martin.* Miss Jackie, 2005.

"Rainstorm." Strausman, Paul. *Blue Jay, Blue Jay!* A Gentle Wind, 1997.

"Rapp Song." Grammer, Red. *Teaching Peace.* Red Note, 1986.

"Rhythm in My Fingers." Gill, Jim. *Moving Rhymes for Modern Times.* Jim Gill, 2006.

"Rise and Shine." McMahon, Elizabeth. *Tea Party Shuffle.* Rosie Rhubarb, 1997.

"Robin Hood." Kirk, John, and Trish Miller. *The Big Rock Candy Mountain.* A Gentle Wind, 2004.

"Rock n' Roll Is Here to Stay." The Learning Station. *Rock n' Roll Songs That Teach.* Monopoli/Learning Station, 1997.

"Rock the Day Away." Fite, Stephen. *Rock the Day Away.* Melody House, 2003.

"R-U-O-K." Magical Music Express. *Friendship Stew.* A Gentle Wind, 2001.

"Saba Il Xheer." Stotts, Stuart. *Are We There Yet?* Tomorrow River, 1991.

"Sailin' Up, Sailin' Down." Seeger, Pete. *Pete Seeger's Family Concert.* Sony, 1992.

"Say Hello." Greg and Steve. *Kidding Around.* Youngheart, 1985.

"Scat like That." Fink, Cathy, and Marcy Marxer. *Scat like That.* Rounder, 2005.

"Scat like That." Greg and Steve. *On the Move.* Youngheart, 1983.

"See-You-Later Song." Parachute Express. *Who's Got a Hug?* Trio Lane, 1998.

"Seeds for My Garden." Grunsky, Jack. *Like a Flower to the Sun*. Casablanca Kids, 2003.

"Seven Days in a Week." Mr. Al and Stephen Fite. *Back to School Again*. Melody House, 1996.

"Shabot Shalom." Jenkins, Ella. *You'll Sing a Song and I'll Sing a Song*. Smithsonian Folkways, 1987.

"Shango." Barchas, Sarah. *Bridges across the World*. High Haven, 1999.

"Shee-nasha." Jenkins, Ella. *Little Johnny Brown*. Smithsonian Folkways, 1971.

"Simone's Song (The Parrot Song)." Gill, Jim. *Jim Gill Sings the Sneezing Song and Other Contagious Tunes*. Jim Gill, 1993.

"Singular and Plural." Feldman, Jean. *Kiss Your Brain*. Jean Feldman, 2003.

"S'mores." Parachute Express. *Doctor Looney's Remedy*. Trio Lane, 1998.

"So Happy You're Here." Palmer, Hap. *So Big*. Hap-Pal, 1994.

"St. Patrick." Cosgrove, Jim. *Bop Bop Dinosaur*. Hiccup, 1998.

"The Stew Song." Simmons, Al. *Something Fishy at Camp Wiganishie*. Casablanca Kids, 1995.

"Super Duper Turbo Toaster Toy Construction Set." Big Jeff. *Big Jeff*. Big Jeff, 2000.

"Super Kid." Kinder, Brian. *One More Time*. Brian Kinder, 2004.

"Swahili Counting Song." The Learning Station. *Literacy in Motion*. Monopoli/Learning Station, 2005.

"The Swing Along Song." Dana. *Dana's Best Sing and Swing-a-Long Tunes*. RMFK, 1997.

"Tahboo." Jenkins, Ella. *Multicultural Children's Songs*. Smithsonian Folkways, 1995.

"Tarzan." Feldman, Jean. *Dr. Jean and Friends*. Jean Feldman, n.d.

"Telephone." Berkner, Laurie. *Buzz Buzz*. Two Tomatoes, 1998.

"Thank You." Barchas, Sarah. *Bridges across the World*. High Haven, 1999.

"There's More to a Seed." Ode, Eric. *Grandpa's Truck*. Deep Rooted, 2003.

"Three Little Sheep." Kinder, Brian. *Again*. Brian Kinder, 2003.

"Toom-Bah-Ee-Lera." Various Artists. *cELLAbration! A Tribute to Ella Jenkins*. Smithsonian Folkways, 2004.

"A Tooty Ta." Mr. Al. *Mr. Al Concert Live*. Cradle Rock, 2004.

"Two Hands Four Hands." Grammer, Red. *Down the Do-Re-Mi*. Red Note, 1991.

"Under One Sky." Pelham, Ruth. *Under One Sky*. A Gentle Wind, 1982.

"Victor Vito." Berkner, Laurie. *Victor Vito*. Two Tomatoes, 1999.

"Wake Up Jacob." Raven, Nancy. *Jambalaya!* Lizard's Rock, 2003.

"Wascawy Wabbit." LaFond, Lois. *One World.* Rockadile, 1989.

"Watch Me." Palmer, Hap. *Sally the Swinging Snake.* Educational Activities, 1987.

"Water Wheel Song." Lonnquist, Ken. *Earthy Songs.* Kenland, 2006.

"We're on Our Way." SteveSongs. *Marvelous Day!* Rounder, 2006.

"We're Talkin' Earthquake!" Raven, Nancy. *Jambalaya!* Lizard's Rock, 2003.

"What a Miracle." Palmer, Hap. *Peek-a-Boo.* Hap-Pal, 1990.

"What You Gonna Wear?" Fink, Cathy, and Marcy Marxer. *Help Yourself.* Rounder, 1990.

"What'll I Do with the Baby-O?" Rosenthal, Phil. *The Green Grass Grew All Around.* American Melody, 1995.

"When a Big Fat Hippopotamus Is Yawning." Barchas, Sarah. *If I Had a Pony.* High Haven, 1996.

"When I Grow Up." Stotts, Stuart, and Tom Pease. *Celebrate: A Song Resource.* Tomorrow River, 2000.

"Where Is Mary?" Jenkins, Ella. *Sharing Cultures with Ella Jenkins.* Smithsonian Folkways, 2003.

"Who Stole the Cookies?" The Learning Station. *Here We Go Loopty Loo.* Monopoli/Learning Station, 1998.

"Yecch!" Alsop, Peter. *Wha' D'Ya Wanna Do?* Moose School, 1983.

"The Yodeling Song." Silberg, "Miss Jackie." *Joining Hands with Other Lands.* Kimbo, 1993.

"You're in the Jug Band." Stotts, Stuart, and Tom Pease. *Celebrate: A Song Resource.* Tomorrow River, 2000.

"Zaminamina." Pease, Tom. *Daddy Starts to Dance.* Tomorrow River, 1996.

Cumulative Songs

Cumulative songs, also known as pattern songs, are fun to use in musical story programs. Many of them are easy to learn because of their repetitive nature. The following songs feature verses that build upon each other.

"All You Et-A." Beall, Pamela, and Susan Nipp. *Wee Sing in the Car*. Price Stern Sloan, 1999.

"The Ants Go Marching." Colleen and Uncle Squaty. *Rumble to the Bottom*. Colleen and Uncle Squaty, 1997.

"Ants in My Pants." Allard, Peter and Ellen. *Pizza Pizzaz*. 80-Z Music, 2006.

"At the Circus." Barchas, Sarah. *If I Had a Pony*. High Haven, 1996.

"Bad Day Today." Del Bianco, Lou. *Lost in School*. Storymaker, 2000.

"A Ballet Dancing Truck Driver." Fink, Cathy, and Marcy Marxer. *Changing Channels*. Rounder, 1996.

"The Barnyard Song." Hinton, Sam. *Whoever Shall Have Some Good Peanuts*. Smithsonian Folkways, 2006.

"Baxter the Bear." Charette, Rick. *Where Do My Sneakers Go at Night?* Pine Point, 1987.

"Birthday Cake." Parachute Express. *Sunny Side Up*. Disney, 1991.

"Black Bat Farm." Peterson, Carole. *H.U.M.—All Year Long*. Macaroni Soup, 2003.

"Blue Jay." Strausman, Paul. *Blue Jay, Blue Jay!* A Gentle Wind, 1997.

"Boom Chica Boom." Feldman, Jean. *Keep on Singing and Dancing with Dr. Jean*. Jean Feldman, 1999.

"Brown Gold." Chapin, Tom. *Some Assembly Required.* Razor & Tie, 2005.

"Bug on the Wall." Allard, Peter and Ellen. *Good Kid.* Peter and Ellen Allard, 2000.

"Button Factory." The Learning Station. *Rock n' Roll Songs That Teach.* Monopoli/Learning Station, 1997.

"Cow in the Car." Dana. *Dana's Best Travelin' Tunes.* RMFK, 1995.

"Down by the Sea." Grammer, Red. *Down the Do-Re-Mi.* Red Note, 1991.

"Drive My Car." Berkner, Laurie. *Under a Shady Tree.* Two Tomatoes, 2002.

"Drivin' in My Car." Ralph's World. *Ralph's World.* Mini Fresh, 2001.

"Driving in My Car." Allard, Peter and Ellen. *Good Kid.* Peter and Ellen Allard, 2000.

"Everybody Clap Your Hands." Peterson, Carole. *Stinky Cake.* Macaroni Soup, 2005.

"Everybody Happy?" Sharon, Lois, and Bram. *Great Big Hits 2.* Elephant, 2002.

"Fantasy Automobile." Parachute Express. *Sunny Side Up.* Disney, 1991.

"Farmer Brown Had Ten Green Apples." Jenkins, Ella. *Growing Up with Ella Jenkins.*

"The Farmer in the Dell." The Learning Station. *All-Time Children's Favorites.* Monopoli/Learning Station, 1993.

"Fiddle I Fee." McMahon, Elizabeth. *Waltzing with Fireflies.* Rosie Rhubarb, 1999.

"The First 12 Days of School." Feldman, Jean. *Keep on Singing and Dancing with Dr. Jean.* Jean Feldman, 1999.

"Five Big Dump Trucks." Beall, Pamela, and Susan Nipp. *Wee Sing in the Car.* Price Stern Sloan, 1999.

"Five Brown Buns." Sharon, Lois, and Bram. *Great Big Hits.* Elephant, 1992.

"Five Little Chickadees." Allard, Peter and Ellen. *Sing It! Say It! Stamp It! Sway It!* vol. 2. 80-Z Music, 1999.

"Five Little Ducks." Trout Fishing in America. *Mine!* Trout, 1994.

"Five Little Frogs." Raffi. *Singable Songs for the Very Young.* Troubadour, 1976.

"Five Little Leaves." Avni, Fran. *Tuning into Nature.* Lemonstone, 2002.

"Five Little Monkeys." Yosi. *Monkey Business.* Yosi, 2002.

"Five Little Pumpkins." Raffi. *Singable Songs for the Very Young.* Troubadour, 1976.

"Flyin' on the Northwind." Tickle Tune Typhoon. *Keep the Spirit.* Music for Little People, 1989.

"Four Little Duckies." Ralph's World. *Ralph's World.* Mini Fresh, 2001.

"Glad to See You." Allard, Peter and Ellen. *Sing It! Say It! Stamp It! Sway It!* vol. 2. 80-Z Music, 1999.

"Go into the Night." Banana Slug String Band. *Penguin Parade*. Music for Little People, 1995.

"Going on a Picnic." Peterson, Carole. *H.U.M.—All Year Long*. Macaroni Soup, 2003.

"Going to Grandma's." Abell, Timmy. *Little Red Wagon*. Upstream, 2005.

"Good-bye, So Long, Farewell, Toodle-oo." Palmer, Hap. *Two Little Sounds*. Hap-Pal, 2003.

"Grandma's House Tonight." Harper, Monty. *Take Me to Your Library*. Monty Harper, 2003.

"Grandmother's Farm." Palmer, Hap. *Witch's Brew*. Educational Activities, 1978.

"Grandpa's Truck." Ode, Eric. *Grandpa's Truck*. Deep Rooted, 2003.

"Great Big Man." Peterson, Carole. *Stinky Cake*. Macaroni Soup, 2005.

"Great Machine." Allard, Peter and Ellen. *Sing It! Say It! Stamp It! Sway It!* vol. 3. 80-Z Music, 2002.

"The Green Grass Grew All Around." Rosenthal, Phil. *The Green Grass Grew All Around*. American Melody, 1995.

"Grey Little Mouse." Allard, Peter and Ellen. *Sing It! Say It! Stamp It! Sway It!* vol. 3. 80-Z Music, 2002.

"Had a Bird." Raven, Nancy. *Hop, Skip, and Sing/Singing in a Circle and Activity Songs*. Lizard's Rock, 2003.

"The Hippopotamus Song." Ode, Eric. *I Love My Shoes*. Deep Rooted, 2005.

"Hole in the Bucket." Petric, Faith. *Sing a Song, Sing Along*. A Gentle Wind, 1982.

"Holey Old Wagon." Haynes, Sammie. *Nature's ABCs*. A Gentle Wind, 2004.

"How I Became a Clown." Chapin, Tom. *Some Assembly Required*. Razor & Tie, 2005.

"Howdja Do That?" Pullara, Steve. *Spinning Tails*. Cool Beans, 2001.

"I Am an Insect." Tickle Tune Typhoon. *Singing Science*. Music for Little People, 2000.

"I Am Here and You Are Here." Allard, Peter and Ellen. *Sing It! Say It! Stamp It! Sway It!* vol. 3. 80-Z Music, 2002.

"I Had a Rooster." Lithgow, John. *Singin' in the Bathtub*. Sony, 1999.

"I Know an Old Lady." Abell, Timmy. *I Know an Old Lady*. Upstream, 1995.

"I Spy." The Learning Station. *Get Funky and Musical Fun*. Monopoli/Learning Station, 2003.

"I Wouldn't Be Scared, Not Me." Stotts, Stuart. *One Big Dance*. Tomorrow River, 1996.

"If You're Happy." Feldman, Jean. *Is Everybody Happy?* Jean Feldman, 2001.

"In My Backyard." Greg and Steve. *Big Fun.* Youngheart, 1997.

"In My Pocket." Charette, Rick. *Chickens on Vacation*. Pine Point, 1990.

"Jelly, Jelly in My Belly." Sharon, Lois, and Bram. *Everybody Sing!* Casablanca Kids, 2002.

"Jumpalong Jake." Chapin, Tom. *Great Big Fun for the Very Little One*. Sundance, 2001.

"Keep Moving." The Learning Station. *Here We Go Loopty Loo*. Monopoli/Learning Station, 1998.

"Keep on Dancing." Avni, Fran. *Artichokes and Brussel Sprouts*. Music for Little People, 1988.

"King Karacticus." Kirk, John, and Trish Miller. *The Big Rock Candy Mountain*. A Gentle Wind, 2004.

"Kiss the Baby Goodnight." Allard, Peter and Ellen. *Sing It! Say It! Stamp It! Sway It!* vol. 3. 80-Z Music, 2002.

"A Little Red Jeep." Charette, Rick. *Toad Motel*. Pine Point, 1999.

"Looking for a Planet." Green Chili Jam Band. *Coconut Moon*. Squeaky Wheel, 1997.

"Milky Way." Harley, Bill. *Down in the Backpack*. Round River, 2001.

"Mockingbird Polka." Fink, Cathy, and Marcy Marxer. *All Wound Up!* Rounder, 2001.

"Mother Gooney Bird." Feldman, Jean. *Dr. Jean and Friends*. Jean Feldman, 1998.

"Must Be Santa." Raffi. *Singable Songs for the Very Young*. Troubadour, 1976.

"My Hands on My Head." Beall, Pamela, and Susan Nipp. *Wee Sing Silly Songs*. Price Stern Sloan, 1982.

"My Mother Is a Baker." Feldman, Jean. *Dr. Jean and Friends*. Jean Feldman, 1998.

"My Old Jalopy." Parachute Express. *Who's Got a Hug?* Trio Lane, 1998.

"My Tooth It Is Wiggling." Allard, Peter and Ellen. *Pizza Pizzaz*. 80-Z Music, 2006.

"Ninety-nine Bottles of Pop." Beall, Pamela, and Susan Nipp. *Wee Sing Silly Songs*. Price Stern Sloan, 1982.

"Nobody Else like Me." Walker, Mary Lu. *The Frog's Party*. A Gentle Wind, 1989.

"Nocturnal." Jonas, Billy. *What Kind of Cat Are You?!* Bang-a-Bucket, 2002.

"Old MacDonald Had a Farm." McGrath, Bob. *Sing Along with Bob #2*. Golden Books, 1990.

"Old Man Noah's Raincoat." Ode, Eric. *Trash Can*. Deep Rooted, 2002.

"On My Birthday." Stotts, Stuart, and Tom Pease. *Celebrate: A Song Resource*. Tomorrow River, 2000.

"Once an Austrian Went Yodeling." Miss Amy. *Wide Wide World*. Ionian, 2005.

"One Finger, One Thumb." Allard, Peter and Ellen. *Sing It! Say It! Stamp It! Sway It!* vol. 1. 80-Z Music, 1999.

"One Little Coyote." Riders in the Sky. *Harmony Ranch*. Sony, 1991.

"Over in the Meadow." McCutcheon, John. *Mail Myself to You*. Rounder, 1988.

"Our School." Barchas, Sarah. *Get Ready, Get Set, Sing!* High Haven, 1994.

"Owl Moon." Pease, Tom. *Daddy Starts to Dance*. Tomorrow River, 1996.

"The Parade Came Marching." Chapin, Tom. *Family Tree*. Sony, 1992.

"Peanut Butter 'n Jelly." Magical Music Express. *Music Is Magic*. Magical Music Express, 2002.

"The Planting Song." Buckner, Janice. *Little Friends for Little Folks*. A Gentle Wind, 1986.

"Rainbow 'round Me." Pelham, Ruth. *Under One Sky*. A Gentle Wind, 1982.

"Rattlin' Bog." Zanes, Dan. *Night Time!* Festival Five, 2002.

"Red Bird." Sharon, Lois, and Bram. *School Days*. Casablanca Kids, 2004.

"Rug in the Middle of the Room." Avni, Fran. *Little Ears: Songs for Reading Readiness*. Leapfrog School House, 2000.

"Sailing to the Sea." Chapin, Tom. *Mother Earth*. Sundance, 1990.

"Seed in the Ground." Kaldor, Connie. *A Duck in New York City*. Folle Avoine, 2003.

"Seven Silly Squirrels." Avni, Fran. *Tuning into Nature*. Lemonstone, 2002.

"Shakin' It." Parachute Express. *Shakin' It!* Disney, 1992.

"She Waded in the Water." Beall, Pamela, and Susan Nipp. *Wee Sing Silly Songs*. Price Stern Sloan, 1982.

"She'll Be Comin' 'round the Mountain." Dana. *Dana's Best Travelin' Tunes*. RMFK, 1995.

"Silly Willy." Feldman, Jean. *Dr. Jean Sings Silly Songs*. Jean Feldman, n.d.

"Singing in the Rain." The Learning Station. *Rock n' Roll Songs That Teach*. Monopoli/Learning Station, 1997.

"Six Little Monkeys." Yosi. *Under a Big Bright Yellow Umbrella*. Yosi, 2004.

"Skidaddle." Howdy, Buck. *Skidaddle!* MCA, 2003.

"Some Houses." Jonas, Billy. *What Kind of Cat Are You?!* Bang-a-Bucket, 2002.

"Something in My Shoe." Raffi. *Rise and Shine.* Troubadour, 1982.

"A Song of One." Chapin, Tom. *Mother Earth.* Sundance, 1990.

"Staple in My Sock." Charette, Rick. *Alligator in the Elevator.* Pine Point, 1985.

"The Stew Song." Simmons, Al. *Something Fishy at Camp Wiganishie.* Casablanca Kids, 1995.

"Super Kid." Kinder, Brian. *One More Time.* Brian Kinder, 2004.

"Ten in the Bed." Allard, Peter and Ellen. *Sing It! Say It! Stamp It! Sway It!* vol. 3. 80-Z Music, 2002.

"Ten Little Kittens/Witches/Turkeys/Snowmen." Barchas, Sarah. *Get Ready, Get Set, Sing!* High Haven, 1994.

"Ten Sleepy Sheep." Harper, Jessica. *40 Winks.* Alacazam, 1998.

"There's a Hole in My Back Yard." Various Artists. *Grandma's Patchwork Quilt.* American Melody, 1987.

"There's a Hole in the Bottom of the Sea." Grammer, Red. *Red Grammer's Favorite Sing Along Songs.* Red Note, 1993.

"There's a Hole in the Bucket." Various Artists. *A Child's Celebration of Silliest Songs.* Music for Little People, 1999.

"There's a Hole in the Middle of the Road." Beall, Pamela, and Susan Nipp. *Wee Sing in the Car.* Price Stern Sloan, 1999.

"There's a Hole in the Middle of the Tree." Avni, Fran. *Tuning into Nature.* Lemonstone, 2002.

"There's a House in the Middle of the Woods." Beall, Pamela, and Susan Nipp. *Wee Sing for Halloween.* Price Stern Sloan, 2002.

"Three Craw." Smith, Tom. *Chip Off the New Block.* A Gentle Wind, 1981.

"Tinkerboxer." Parachute Express. *Friends, Forever Friends.* Trio Lane, 1996.

"Today Is Monday." Beall, Pamela, and Susan Nipp. *Wee Sing Sing-Alongs.* Price Stern Sloan, 1982.

"A Tooty Ta." Mr. Al. *Mr. Al Concert Live.* Cradle Rock, 2004.

"The Train Song." Buckner, Janice. *Little Friends for Little Folks.* A Gentle Wind, 1986.

"Uncle Squaty Went Yodeling." Colleen and Uncle Squaty. *Fingerplays, Movement and Story Songs.* Colleen and Uncle Squaty, 1993.

"Walking in the Woods." Barchas, Sarah. *If I Had a Pony.* High Haven, 1996.

"What Do You Hear?" Coffey, James. *My Mama Was a Train*. Blue Vision, 2002.

"What Will I Take to the Moon?" Parachute Express. *Happy to Be Here*. Disney, 1991.

"What's on the List." Fite, Stephen. *Gobs of Fun*. Melody House, 2005.

"When a Big Fat Hippopotamus Is Yawning." Barchas, Sarah. *If I Had a Pony*. High Haven, 1996.

"When I First Came to This Land." Colleen and Uncle Squaty. *1, 2, 3, Four-Ever Friends*. Colleen and Uncle Squaty, 1995.

"Who's Been Sleeping in My Bed?" Fink, Cathy, and Marcy Marxer. *Pocket Full of Stardust*. Rounder, 2002.

"Whoever Shall Have Some Good Peanuts." Hinton, Sam. *Whoever Shall Have Some Good Peanuts*. Smithsonian Folkways, 2006.

"Wiggle in My Toe." Scruggs, Joe. *Late Last Night*. Educational Graphics, 1984.

"World of Make Believe." Parachute Express. *Feel the Music*. Disney, 1991.

Songs Sung in Rounds

A round is a song where two or more voices sing the same lines in a song, but each voice starts its line at a different time. Rounds are good songs to share with groups of children when you have time to rehearse them.

"All around the World." Fink, Cathy, and Marcy Marxer. *Pillow Full of Wishes*. Rounder, 2000.

"America, America." Beall, Pamela, and Susan Nipp. *Wee Sing America*. Price Stern Sloan, 1987.

"Arirang." Raven, Nancy. *Friends and Family*. Lizard's Rock, 2003.

"The Beach Song." Magical Music Express. *Music Is Magic*. Magical Music Express, 2002.

"Bedtime Round." Chapin, Tom. *Billy the Squid*. Sony, 1992.

"Belly Button (Round)." Boynton, Sandra. *Philadelphia Chickens*. Boynton, 2002.

"The Black Bat Sat." Beall, Pamela, and Susan Nipp. *Wee Sing for Halloween*. Price Stern Sloan, 2002.

"Black Socks." Harley, Bill. *Play It Again*. Round River, 1999.

"Can You Dig That Crazy Jibberish." Smith, Tom. *Chip Off the New Block*. A Gentle Wind, 1981.

"Catches." Chapin, Tom. *Moonboat*. Sundance, 1989.

"Chairs to Mend." Beall, Pamela, and Susan Nipp. *Wee Sing Sing-Alongs*. Price Stern Sloan, 1982.

"Christmas Is Here." Raven, Nancy. *Sky Bears/Songs for the Holidays*. Lizard's Rock, 2003.

"Come Follow." Sharon, Lois, and Bram. *Everybody Sing!* Casablanca Kids, 2002.

"Creeping, Creeping." Beall, Pamela, and Susan Nipp. *Wee Sing for Halloween*. Price Stern Sloan, 2002.

"Dinosaur Round." Boynton, Sandra. *Rhinoceros Tap*. Boynton, 1996.

"'Doo-Doo' Is a Bad Word." Polisar, Barry Louis. *Juggling Babies*. Rainbow Morning, 1993.

"Down by the Station." Sharon, Lois, and Bram. *Great Big Hits*. Elephant, 1992.

"Fish and Chips and Vinegar." Sharon, Lois, and Bram. *Great Big Hits*. Elephant, 1992.

"Frère Jacques." Williams, Robin and Linda. *Down in the Valley*. A Gentle Wind, 1982.

"The Frog in the Bog." Beall, Pamela, and Susan Nipp. *Wee Sing Fun 'n' Folk*. Price Stern Sloan, 1989.

"Frog Round." Beall, Pamela, and Susan Nipp. *Wee Sing Sing-Alongs*. Price Stern Sloan, 1982.

"The Frog's Song." Magical Music Express. *Friendship Stew*. A Gentle Wind, 2001.

"Grasshoppers Three." Beall, Pamela, and Susan Nipp. *Wee Sing Fun 'n' Folk*. Price Stern Sloan, 1989.

"Grow in Your Own Way." Chapin, Tom. *Moonboat*. Sundance, 1989.

"Have You Seen the Ghost of John?" Beall, Pamela, and Susan Nipp. *Wee Sing for Halloween*. Price Stern Sloan, 2002.

"Hey Ho! Nobody Home." Beall, Pamela, and Susan Nipp. *Wee Sing Sing-Alongs*. Price Stern Sloan, 1982.

"I Love the Mountains." Byers, Kathy. *'Round the Campfire*. KT Music, 2004.

"Kookaburra." Staines, Bill. *The Happy Wanderer*. Red House, 1993.

"Let Us Sing Together." Beall, Pamela, and Susan Nipp. *Wee Sing Sing-Alongs*. Price Stern Sloan, 1982.

"Little Tommy Tinker." Sharon, Lois, and Bram. *Name Games*. Casablanca Kids, 2002.

"Make New Friends." Sweet Honey in the Rock. *All for Freedom*. Music for Little People, 1989.

"Matthew, Mark, Luke and John." Herdman, Priscilla. *Stardreamer*. Alacazam, 1988.

"Oh How Lovely Is the Evening." Barchas, Sarah. *Bridges across the World*. High Haven, 1999.

"One Earth." Arnold, Linda. *Happiness Cake*. Ariel, 1988.

"One More Round." Harper, Jessica. *A Wonderful Life*. Alacazam, 1994.

"Peace Round." Pease, Tom. *Boogie! Boogie! Boogie!* Tomorrow River, 1986.

"A Ram Sam Sam." Beall, Pamela, and Susan Nipp. *Wee Sing Sing-Alongs*. Price Stern Sloan, 1982.

"Reuben and Rachel." Beall, Pamela, and Susan Nipp. *Wee Sing Sing-Alongs*. Price Stern Sloan, 1982.

"Rounds." Chapin, Tom. *Family Tree*. Sony, 1992.

"Row, Row, Row Your Boat." Beall, Pamela, and Susan Nipp. *Wee Sing Sing-Alongs*. Price Stern Sloan, 1982.

"Russian Lullaby." The Chenille Sisters. *1 2 3 for Kids*. Red House, 1990.

"Scotland's Burning." Beall, Pamela, and Susan Nipp. *Wee Sing Sing-Alongs*. Price Stern Sloan, 1982.

"Seasons." Magical Music Express. *Music Is Magic*. Magical Music Express, 2002.

"Sing a Round." Magical Music Express. *Music Is Magic*. Magical Music Express, 2002.

"Sing Together." Beall, Pamela, and Susan Nipp. *Wee Sing Sing-Alongs*. Price Stern Sloan, 1982.

"Slimy Mud." Magical Music Express. *Music Is Magic*. Magical Music Express, 2002.

"Sweet Potato Round." Raven, Nancy. *Jambalaya!* Lizard's Rock, 2003.

"Sweetly Sings the Donkey." Beall, Pamela, and Susan Nipp. *Wee Sing Animals, Animals, Animals*. Price Stern Sloan, 1999.

"Tender Shepherd." McCutcheon, John. *Howjadoo*. Rounder, 1986.

"There Is Thunder." Beall, Pamela, and Susan Nipp. *Wee Sing Children's Songs and Fingerplays*. Price Stern Sloan, 1977.

"This Pretty Planet." Chapin, Tom. *This Pretty Planet*. Sony, 2000.

"This Pretty Planet II." Chapin, Tom. *This Pretty Planet*. Sony, 2000.

"Three Blind Mice." Beall, Pamela, and Susan Nipp. *Wee Sing Sing-Alongs*. Price Stern Sloan, 1982.

"Tue Tue." Harley, Bill. *There's a Pea on My Plate*. Round River, 1997.

"The Upward Trail." Beall, Pamela, and Susan Nipp. *Wee Sing in the Car*. Price Stern Sloan, 1999.

"White Coral Bells." Berkner, Laurie. *Victor Vito*. Two Tomatoes, 1999.

"Why Shouldn't My Goose?" Beall, Pamela, and Susan Nipp. *Wee Sing Sing-Alongs*. Price Stern Sloan, 1982.

"Wild Bird Round." Lonnquist, Ken. *Earthy Songs*. Kenland, 2006.

The Best Picture Books Featuring Music in Your Library

The three following annotated bibliographies feature the best children's picture books that feature music and dance. These select lists contain only books that were in print at the time of this writing.

PICTURE BOOKS BASED ON SONG LYRICS

There are a surprising number of picture books whose text is made up of original and traditional children's songs (and sometimes adult songs packaged for children). Many of the books are straight visual interpretations of songs. Some books add new verses, and other books are parodies, replacing the old words with new, humorous words. Some picture books include a musical score or chords or both, usually in the back matter or sometimes on the endpapers. These have been noted in the annotations.

Ajhar, Brian. *Home on the Range*. Dial, 2004.

> A city kid sees antelope playing in the clouds and cowboy-hat constellations at night. His rocking horse takes him zooming into the air. He frolics with cattle for awhile before heading back to his western-themed bedroom. Score and chords included. The song "Home on the Range" can be found on the recording *The Happy Wanderer* by Bill Staines (Red House, 1993).

Arnold, Tedd. *Catalina Magdalena Hoopensteiner Wallendiner Hogan Logan Bogan Was Her Name*. Scholastic, 2004.

> A girl with an unusually long name goes from infancy through her school years and works as a grown-up in a fish factory. She eventually gets married

to a guy named Smith. Score and chords included. A version titled "Patalina Matalina" can be found on the recording *Dr. Jean and Friends* by Jean Feldman (Jean Feldman, 1998).

Autry, Gene, and Oakley Haldeman. *Here Comes Santa Claus.* **Illustrated by Bruce Whatley. HarperCollins, 2002.**

"Here comes Santa Claus! Here comes Santa Claus! Right down Santa Claus Lane!" A little puppy sneaks aboard Santa's sleigh on Christmas Eve in this interpretation of Gene Autry's Christmas classic. Santa discovers the stowaway and leaves it for a little boy as his Christmas present. Score and chords included. Autry's version can be found on his recording *Rudolph the Red-Nosed Reindeer and Other Christmas Classics* (Sony, 2003).

Bates, Ivan. *Five Little Ducks.* **Orchard, 2006.**

Five little ducks wander away from their mother, one by one. The first duck stops to visit a beaver. The subsequent ducks visit a cow, a crab, a rabbit, and a goat. The little ducks eventually return to their mother with tiny gifts. Score and chords included. A version of "Five Little Ducks" can be found on the recording *Get Ready, Get Set, Sing!* by Sarah Barchas (High Haven, 1994).

Bates, Katherine Lee. *America the Beautiful.* **Illustrated by Neil Waldman. Atheneum, 1993.**

The opening lines of the song are paired with an illustration of Niagara Falls. Other natural wonders featured include the Grand Tetons, the Great Plains, the Grand Canyon, Mesa Verde, the Coastal Redwoods, Pike's Peak, Mount Rushmore, the Statue of Liberty, and more. Score included. The song can be found on the recording *America the Beautiful* by the Twin Sisters (Twin Sisters, 2005).

Baum, Maxie. *I Have a Little Dreidel.* **Illustrated by Julie Paschkis. Scholastic, 2006.**

A family gathers to celebrate Hanukkah. They make latkes, light candles, feast, and then clean up. The adults dance and make music while the children play with the dreidel. Score and chords included. A version of the song can be found as "My Dreydel" on the recording *Singable Songs for the Very Young* by Raffi (Troubadour, 1976).

Belafonte, Harry, and Lord Burgess. *Island in the Sun.* **Illustrated by Alex Ayliffe. Dial, 1999.**

This is an ode to island life. "Where my people have toiled since time begun / Tho I may sail on many a sea, / Her shores will always be home to me." The images show the island inhabitants working, going to the open market, and celebrating with drums and dance. Score and chords included. The song can be found on the recording *All-Time Greatest Hits*, vol. 1, by Harry Belafonte (RCA, 1978).

Berkner, Laurie. *Victor Vito and Freddie Vasco.* **Illustrated by Henry Cole. Scholastic, 2004.**

Two Alaskan polar bears temporarily close their restaurant, the Klondike Café, and travel in search of new foods to serve. They tour the United States and load their car with ingredients for rice and beans, rutabagas and collard greens, and spaghetti. Score, chords, and CD included.

Birdseye, Tom, and Debbie Holsclaw Birdseye. *She'll Be Comin' round the Mountain.* **Illustrated by Andrew Glass. Holiday House, 1994.**

Opa and Oma are delighted to find that Tootie is coming for a visit. They start singing the title song for their young ones. Tootie will "drive her old jalopy when she comes," wear jeans and slop boots, and bring her old pig Clovis and the rest of her farm critters "when she comes." Score and chords included. A version of "She'll Be Comin' 'round the Mountain" can be found on the recording *Whaddaya Think of That?* by Laurie Berkner (Two Tomatoes, 2000).

Brett, Jan. *The Twelve Days of Christmas.* **Putnam, 1986.**

The center picture of each double-page spread shows the succession of gifts from the song. The borders show a man and his family going into the woods, chopping down a Christmas tree, and decorating it. Different animals also appear in the borders displaying ways to say "Merry Christmas" in foreign languages. Score included. The song can be found on the recording *A Very Merry Kidz Bop* by the Kidz Bop Kids (Razor & Tie, 2005).

Brown, Rick. *Old MacDonald Had a Cow.* **Sterling, 2005.**

Old MacDonald milks his cow "with a pull-pull here and a pull-pull there." We also meet his cat, dog, pony, lamb, piglet, goat, and two children. The only thing missing is the "E-I-E-I-O" refrain. The cow illustrations are textured for a tactile experience. A version of "Old MacDonald" can be found on the recording *Get Ready, Get Set, Sing!* by Sarah Barchas (High Haven, 1994).

Cabrera, Jane. *If You're Happy and You Know It!* **Holiday House, 2005.**

A group of animals encourages the readers to demonstrate their happiness by clapping, stamping, nodding, roaring, spinning, kissing, flapping, squeaking, and jumping. In the end, the animals show they are happy by shouting, "We are!" A version of the song can be found on the recording *Happiness Cake* by Linda Arnold (Ariel, 1988).

Cabrera, Jane. *Over in the Meadow.* **Holiday House, 1999.**

Cabrera begins her version of the traditional song with Old Mother Turtle and her little turtle One. She continues this counting book with two young fish, three owls, four rats, five bees, six ducks, seven froggies, eight lizards, nine worms, and ten rabbits. A version of "Over in the Meadow" can be found on the recording *Mail Myself to You* by John McCutcheon (Rounder, 1988).

Cabrera, Jane. *Ten in the Bed.* **Holiday House, 2006.**

Ten little animals knock each other off the bed, one by one, until only the Little One is left. When he falls off the bed, the animals all dance about. They settle down back in bed and "the Little One said . . . 'Good night!'" The song "Ten in the Bed" can be found on the recording *Sleepytime* by Sharon, Lois, and Bram (Casablanca Kids, 2002).

Carle, Eric. *Today Is Monday.* **Putnam, 1993.**

Several colorful animals eat a variety of food while children learn the days of the week. Most of the animals eat human food; a snake eats string beans, and a monkey eats an ice-cream cone. There are, however, a pelican eating a whole fish and a fox carrying off a live chicken. Score and chords included. A version of the song can be found on the recording *Wee Sing Sing-Alongs* by Pamela Beall and Susan Nipp (Price Stern Sloan, 1982).

Child, Lydia Maria. *Over the River: A Turkey's Tale.* **Illustrated by Derek Anderson. Simon & Schuster, 2005.**

A family of turkeys heads out to visit Grandma and Grandpa in this takeoff of the classic Thanksgiving song. Along the way, they are pursued by a boy and his dog. The turkeys are rescued by the horse that "knows the way to carry the sleigh." This horse literally carries the sleigh under his arm. Score and chords included. A recording of "Over the River and Through the Woods" can be found on *The Green Grass Grew All Around* by Phil Rosenthal (American Melody, 1995).

Church, Caroline Jayne. *Do Your Ears Hang Low?* **Scholastic, 2002.**

Two dogs with unusually long ears cavort on a hilltop. Their ears correspond with the song lyrics. The book culminates with a large foldout page featuring both dogs making an intertwining heart shape with their ears. A version of "Do Your Ears Hang Low?" can be found on the recording *Great Big Hits 2* by Sharon, Lois, and Bram (Elephant, 2002).

Cohan, George M. *You're a Grand Old Flag.* Illustrated by Todd Ouren. Picture Window Books, 2003.

Images of the American flag are seen in many double-page illustrations. Betsy Ross is shown sewing a flag, a ship is flying the flag, and it also appears with Abraham Lincoln, in a schoolyard, at a town square, on the side of a barn, and in a military procession. Score included. The song can be found on the recording *Wee Sing America* by Pamela Beall and Susan Nipp (Price Stern Sloan, 1987). Other books in the Picture Window Patriotic series include

> Bates, Katherine Lee. *America the Beautiful* (2003)
>
> Gilmore, Patrick S. *When Johnny Comes Marching Home* (2005)
>
> Key, Francis Scott. *The Star Spangled Banner* (2004)
>
> Smith, Samuel Francis. *America My Country 'Tis of Thee* (2003)
>
> *Yankee Doodle* (2003)

Colandro, Lucille. *There Was an Old Lady Who Swallowed a Bat.* Illustrated by Jared Lee. Scholastic, 2002.

This Halloween version of "I Know an Old Lady" finds a woman swallowing a bat, owl, cat, ghost, goblin, and bones. She finally swallows a wizard, who casts a spell that allows the lady to yell, "Trick or treat." All of the creatures come out in one final burp. A version of "I Know an Old Lady" can be found on the recording *I Know an Old Lady* by Timmy Abell (Upstream, 1995).

Conahan, Carolyn. *The Twelve Days of Christmas Dogs.* Dutton, 2005.

A girl gets "a pug puppy under the tree." Then she gets two turtle dogs (dogs in turtleneck sweaters), three French dogs (poodles), four collie dogs, five golden dogs, and so on. They all put on a circus show at the end. The traditional song can be found on the recording *A Very Merry Kidz Bop* by the Kidz Bop Kids (Razor & Tie, 2005).

Crebbin, June. *Cows in the Kitchen.* Illustrated by Katharine McEwen. Scholastic, 1998.

Several cows are seen trashing the farmhouse kitchen to the tune of "Skip to My Lou." Other animals invade the house. Pigs are in the pantry, sheep are on the sofa, and more. Where's Tom Farmer? Asleep in the haystack. The song can be found on the recording *Little Ears: Songs for Reading Readiness* by Fran Avni (Leapfrog School House, 2000).

Cummings, Pat. *My Aunt Came Back.* HarperCollins, 1998.

The narrator's aunt returns from Bucharest with a quilted vest, from Pakistan with a painted fan, from Montreal with a parasol, from old Beijing with a golden ring, and from Mandalay with a red beret. She's next heading to Katmandu and takes the narrator, too, in this short board book. A similar version can be found on the recording *Wee Sing in the Car* by Pamela Beall and Susan Nipp (Price Stern Sloan, 1999).

Eagle, Kin. *It's Raining, It's Pouring.* Illustrated by Rob Gilbert. Whispering Coyote, 1994.

The old man is snoring while it's raining outside (and raining through several leaks in his roof). The old man is also sneezy when it's breezy, growing when it's snowing, and trying to get honey when it's sunny. We also learn his name is Willy when it's chilly, and his wife's name is Cindy when it's windy. Score included. The traditional version can be found on the recording *Songs and Games for Toddlers* by Bob McGrath and Katherine Smithrim (Kids' Records, 1985).

Ehrhardt, Karen. *This Jazz Man.* Illustrated by R. G. Roth. Harcourt, 2006.

The text follows the pattern of the traditional song "This Old Man" and introduces the reader to famous jazz musicians through history, such as Louis Armstrong, Bill "Bojangles" Robinson, Charlie Parker, and Dizzy Gillespie. "This jazz man, he plays one / He plays rhythm with his thumb." The tune of "This Old Man" can be found on several recordings, including the recording *Baby Beluga* by Raffi (Troubadour, 1980).

Farjeon, Eleanor. *Morning Has Broken.* Illustrated by Tim Ladwig. Eerdmans, 1996.

Musician Cat Stevens made this song popular in the 1970s, but few people are aware that Farjeon, a children's author, wrote the words in the early 1900s. Ladwig uses interesting perspectives as we watch a boy, an older man, and a red-winged blackbird celebrate the wonders of a new day. Score included. The song can be found on the recording *Greatest Hits* by Cat Stevens (A&M, 1983).

Fitzgerald, Ella, and Van Alexander. *A-Tisket, A-Tasket.* Illustrated by Ora Eitan. Philomel, 2003.

A baseball-cap-wearing child loses a yellow basket while petting a dog. A little girl finds it and heads to the market. The first child has a fit and searches the city for the basket. The two children, the dog, and the basket finally get together in a park. The song can be found sung by Fitzgerald on many of her recordings, including *Pure Ella* (Verve, 1997).

Garcia, Jerry, and David Grisman. *There Ain't No Bugs on Me.* **Illustrated by Bruce Whatley. HarperCollins, 1999.**

Whatley features a couple of guitar-playing bears; one looks suspiciously like Jerry Garcia. The bears travel all over, accompanied by bugs, before ending up on a small concert stage. CD included.

Garriel, Barbara S. *I Know a Shy Fellow Who Swallowed a Cello.* **Illustrated by John O'Brien. Boyds Mill, 2004.**

Not only does the shy fellow swallow a cello, he also swallows a harp, a fiddle, a cymbal, a flute, a kazoo, and a bell in this spoof of the song "I Know an Old Lady." Once the fellow swallows the bell, his belly wiggles and shakes, and he spits out the instruments, one by one. A version of "I Know an Old Lady" can be found on the recording *Here We Go Loopty Loo* by the Learning Station (Monopoli/Learning Station, 1998).

Gershwin, George, Dubose and Dorothy Heyward, and Ira Gershwin. *Summertime from Porgy and Bess.* **Illustrated by Mike Wimmer. Simon & Schuster, 1999.**

A rural family enjoys swimming, fishing, stretching out on a hammock, working in the field, and attending church during the summer months. Wimmer's rich oil paintings look like photographs with their detail and expressions. Score and chords included. The song can be found on the original soundtrack of *Porgy and Bess* (BMG, 1999).

Gill, Jim. *May There Always Be Sunshine.* **Illustrated by Susie Signorino-Richards. Jim Gill Books, 2001.**

Gill extends the lyrics of this popular Russian song with other things children hope for. "May there always be pancakes" is just one example, along with books, blankets, farmers, hats, rain, and ending with "May there always be us." Score and chords included. Gill's version can be found on his recordings *Jim Gill Sings the Sneezing Song and Other Contagious Tunes* (Jim Gill, 1993) and *Jim Gill's Irrational Anthem* (Jim Gill, 2001).

Greene, Carol. *The 13 Days of Halloween.* **Illustrated by Tim Raglin. Bridgewater, 2000.**

"On the first day of Halloween, my good friend gave to me a vulture in a dead tree." So goes this Halloween parody of "The Twelve Days of Christmas." Other gifts include two hissing cats, three fat toads, four giggling ghosts, five cooked worms, and so on. The traditional "The Twelve Days of Christmas" can be found on the recording *A Very Merry Kidz Bop* by the Kidz Bop Kids (Razor & Tie, 2005).

Guthrie, Woody. *Bling Blang.* **Illustrated by Vladimir Radunsky. Candlewick, 2000.**

A couple of kids and a few animals use a hammer, saw, and building materials to "build a house for the baby-o." The last few pages of the book feature children's drawings of houses. "Bling Blang" can be found on Guthrie's recording *Woody's 20 Grow Big Songs* (Warner Brothers, 1992). Other Radunsky interpretations of Guthrie songs for Candlewick include *Howdi Do* (2000) and *My Dolly* (2001).

Guthrie, Woody. *New Baby Train.* **Illustrated by Marla Frazee. Little, Brown, 2004.**

Where do babies come from? Why, the baby train, of course. The babies ride the train, wondering where they are going to get off. After the babies travel over rivers, mountains, and "through the sky and everywhere else," they find their homes and families. Kim Wilson sings the song on the Guthrie tribute recording *Daddy-o-Daddy* (Rounder, 2001).

Hale, Sarah Josepha. *Mary Had a Little Lamb.* **Illustrated by Sally Mavor. Orchard, 1995.**

Mavor's fabric relief artwork shows a rural passing of the seasons, first with the lamb in a barn stall, then in the family home, next frolicking with Mary and her family, and finally hiding beneath her school desk. The lamb looks sad when "the teacher turned it out" but happy when Mary rejoins the lamb after school. A version of the song can be found on the recording *The Paw Paw Patch* by Phil Rosenthal (American Melody, 1987).

Harley, Bill. *Sittin' Down to Eat.* **Illustrated by Kitty Harvill. August House, 1996.**

Several large animals, including an elephant, a tiger, and a whale, all squeeze into a boy's home. The house finally explodes with a "BOOM!" when a tiny caterpillar joins them. The song can be found on the recording *Play It Again* by Bill Harley (Round River, 1999).

Harper, Charise Mericle. *There Was a Bold Lady Who Wanted a Star.* **Little, Brown, 2002.**

The bold lady wishes for a star. She buys some running shoes but fails to reach the star. In succession, she tries skating, riding a bike, driving a car, and flying an airplane before finally buying a rocket. She sticks the star into a jar "so it wasn't so far." A version of "I Know an Old Lady" can be found on the recording *Here We Go Loopty Loo* by the Learning Station (Monopoli/Learning Station, 1998).

Harper, Jessica. *Four Boys Named Jordan.* **Illustrated by Tara Calahan King. Putnam, 2004.**

Elizabeth the narrator complains when a fourth boy named Jordan joins the classroom. Roll call is a mess when the teacher "asks if Jordan's present." Things get worse when the class gets a new girl. Her name? Jordan! The song can be found on the recording *Inside Out* by Jessica Harper (Rounder, 2001).

Harper, Jessica. *I'm Not Going to Chase the Cat Today!* **Illustrated by Lindsay Harper duPont. HarperCollins, 2000.**

A dog wakes up one day and decides to change his routine by not chasing the cat. The cat in turn decides not to chase the mouse. The mouse, wearing a T-shirt featuring a wedge of cheese, refrains from chasing the lady. The lady throws a party and invites the dog, cat, and mouse. The song can be found on the recording *Rhythm in My Shoes* by Jessica Harper (Rounder, 2000).

Harper, Jessica. *Lizzy's Do's and Don'ts.* **Illustrated by Lindsay Harper duPont. HarperCollins, 2002.**

Lizzy's mother recites a long list of rules, such as "Don't put 10 Band-Aids on your knees." Lizzie says that it's her turn, and she gives her mother a list of rules, such as "Don't make me wear that yellow dress." The two of them finally come up with lists of "Do's," such as "Do ask me if I love you." The song can be found on the recording *Inside Out* by Jessica Harper (Rounder, 2001).

Harper, Jessica. *Nora's Room.* **Illustrated by Lindsay Harper duPont. HarperCollins, 2001.**

Mom, who is downstairs, hears an incredible amount of noise coming from Nora's room. It sounds like bears dancing with moose, as well as "47 monkeys are talking on the phone." In the end, Nora replies that nothing is going on. The song can be found on the recording *Nora's Room* by Jessica Harper (Alacazam, 1996).

Hillenbrand, Will. *Down by the Station.* **Harcourt, 1999.**

A train travels through the zoo and picks up young zoo animals that are waiting patiently by the tracks with their animal parents. The train delivers them to the Children's Zoo, where they play with human children. Score included. A version of the song can be found on the recording *My Mama Was a Train* by James Coffey (Blue Vision, 2002).

Hillenbrand, Will. *Fiddle-I-Fee.* **Harcourt, 2002.**

Two farmers perform their chores through the seasons. Every double-page spread shows the various farm animals playing musical instruments in the barn at night. The last page features the farmers and their baby "under yonder tree." Score included. "Fiddle I Fee" can be found on the recording *Waltzing with Fireflies* by Elizabeth McMahon (Rosie Rhubarb, 1999).

Hillenbrand, Will. *Here We Go round the Mulberry Bush.* **Harcourt, 2003.**

A little piggy child is nervous on her first day of school. New lyrics extend the whole school experience from "Here is where we hang our hat" to "This is how we clean our room." In the end, of course, the little pig is excited about returning to school the next day. Score included. A version titled "Mulberry Bush" can be found on the recording *Seasonal Songs in Motion* by the Learning Station (Monopoli/Learning Station, 2001).

Hoberman, Mary Ann. *Bill Grogan's Goat.* **Illustrated by Nadine Bernard Westcott. Little, Brown, 2002.**

The original song finds the goat eating red shirts off a clothesline, getting tied to a railroad track, and then coughing up the shirts to warn an approaching train to stop. In Hoberman's extended story line, the goat boards the train and meets the engineer, a sheep, a pig, and a cow. Score included. The song can be found on the recording *Wee Sing Silly Songs* by Pamela Beall and Susan Nipp (Price Stern Sloan, 1982). Hoberman and Westcott teamed up on several song lyric picture books for Little, Brown, including

> *The Eensy Weensy Spider* (2000)
>
> *Mary Had a Little Lamb* (2003)
>
> *There Was an Old Man Named Michael Finnegan* (2001)
>
> *Yankee Doodle* (2004)

Holiday, Billie, and Arthur Herzog Jr. *God Bless the Child.* **Illustrated by Jerry Pinkney. HarperCollins, 2004.**

Pinkney uses the Great Migration of African Americans moving from the rural South to northern cities as the backdrop to the Billie Holiday classic song. A sharecropper family packs up their car and adjusts to their new home in Chicago. CD included. Holiday's version can be found on the recording *God Bless the Child: The Very Best of Billie Holiday* (Sony, 2006).

Hoose, Phillip and Hannah. *Hey, Little Ant.* **Illustrated by Debbie Tilley. Tricycle Press, 1998.**

An ant pleads with a boy who is about to squish it. The ant tells the boy that its nest mates need him because he's strong and he helps feeds baby ants. The lyrics end asking the reader if the boy should squish the ant or not. Score and chords included.

Hort, Lenny. *The Seals on the Bus.* **Illustrated by G. Brian Karas. Holt, 2000.**

Seals go traveling to the tune of "The Wheels on the Bus." Other critters pile on the bus, including geese, rabbits, monkeys, vipers, sheep, and skunks. In the end, the people on the bus go "Help, Help, Help!" (or at least, the adults do). "The Wheels on the Bus" can be found on the recording *Travelin' Magic* by Joanie Bartels (BMG, 1988).

Hudson, Wade and Cheryl. *How Sweet the Sound: African-American Songs for Children.* **Illustrated by Floyd Cooper. Scholastic, 1995.**

Starting with the traditional "Kum Ba Ya," the Hudsons look at African American spirituals, street cries, show tunes, the blues, jazz numbers, hand-clapping songs, and more. Scores and chords included.

Hurd, Thatcher. *Mama Don't Allow.* **HarperCollins, 1984.**

Miles forms the Swamp Band, and they are invited to play on a riverboat filled with alligators. They escape when they learn that the Swamp Band is on the menu. The traditional version of "Mama Don't Allow" can be found on the recording *Every Day Is a Birthday* by Brady Rymer (Bumblin' Bee, 2006).

Jackson, Alison. *I Know an Old Lady Who Swallowed a Pie.* **Illustrated by Judith Byron Schachner. Dutton, 1997.**

An old lady swallows an entire pie at Thanksgiving time. As a result, she swallows some cider to moisten the pie, a roll to go with the cider, a squash, a salad, a turkey, a pot, a ten-layer cake, and bread. She becomes so huge that she's used as a float in a Thanksgiving Day parade. A version of "I Know an Old Lady" can be found on the recording *I Know an Old Lady* by Timmy Abell (Upstream, 1995).

Joel, Billy. *New York State of Mind.* **Illustrated by Izak. Scholastic, 2005.**

A little dog takes a Greyhound bus into New York City to see the sights, including Times Square, Central Park, and Chinatown. The funniest illustration shows the dog waiting in line for a performance of the Billy Joel and Twyla Tharp production of *Movin' Out.* CD included.

Johnson, James Weldon. *Lift Ev'ry Voice and Sing.* **Illustrated by Jan Spivey Gilchrist. Scholastic, 1995.**

Gilchrist's illustrations open with an image of a personified Africa, weeping and spilling tears into the ocean. The water imagery continues throughout the book until the end, when several people are seen flying through the air. Score included. The song can be found on the recording *Lift Every Voice* by the Mark Lomax Trio (Blacklisted Musik, 2004).

Johnson, Paul Brett. *Little Bunny Foo Foo.* **Scholastic, 2004.**

Little Bunny Foo Foo bops field mice on the head with mud pies and moves on to teasing woodchucks, foxes, and grizzly bears. As punishment for his misdeeds, the Good Fairy turns Little Bunny Foo Foo into a Goon. Score included. A version titled "Little Rabbit Foo Foo" can be found on the recording *Great Big Hits* by Sharon, Lois, and Bram (Elephant, 1992).

Johnson, Paul Brett. *On Top of Spaghetti.* **Scholastic, 2006.**

A mouse cook sneezes from too much pepper, and a meatball goes flying through town and under a bush. The bush grows into a tree that grows meatballs and tomato sauce, much to the delight of the canine restaurant owner. Score included. The song can be found on the recording *What's Eatin' Yosi?* by Yosi (Yosi, 2006).

Jones, Carol. *This Old Man.* **Houghton Mifflin, 1990.**

Die-cut holes give clues to what the old man plays with his drumsticks in this adaptation of the traditional song. The first scene features "One" and shows that the old man "played knick knack on my . . ." The die-cut hole shows a picture of a drum. Score and chords included. The song can be found on the recording *Artichokes and Brussel Sprouts* by Fran Avni (Music for Little People, 1988).

Katz, Alan. *Take Me Out of the Bathtub and Other Silly Dilly Songs.* **Illustrated by David Catrow. Margaret K. McElderry, 2001.**

The title song is sung to "Take Me Out to the Ballgame." Other highlights include "Give Me a Break" sung to "Home on the Range," in which the singer's library book "was due back in '92," and the slightly gross "Stinky, Stinky Diaper Change" sung to "Twinkle, Twinkle, Little Star." Other books by Katz in the series include

> *Are You Quite Polite?* (2006)
>
> *I'm Still Here in the Bathtub* (2003)
>
> *Where Did They Hide My Presents?* (2005)

Kaye, Buddy, Fred Wise, and Sidney Lippman. *A You're Adorable.* **Illustrated by Martha Alexander. Candlewick, 1994.**

Little children play together and celebrate life in this alphabet book based on the popular song from the 1940s. "Alphabetically speaking, you're okay." Score included. The song can be found on the recording *Great Big Hits* by Sharon, Lois, and Bram (Elephant, 1992).

Keats, Ezra Jack. *The Little Drummer Boy.* **Viking, 1968.**

A young boy follows the three wise men and their caravan to see Baby Jesus in the manger. The boy is sad because he's poor. "I have no gift to bring." Mary lets him know that he can play his drums. Score included. The song can be found on the recording *Christmas Favorites* (Music for Little People, 1998).

Kellogg, Steven. *A-Hunting We Will Go!* **Morrow, 1998.**

Two kids and their teddy bears make one last imaginative hunt before bedtime. They meet many animals on their journey before donning their pajamas, reading books, and climbing into bed. Score and chords included. The song can be found on *Whoever Shall Have Some Good Peanuts* by Sam Hinton (Smithsonian Folkways, 2006).

Kellogg, Steven. *Give the Dog a Bone.* **Seastar Books, 2000.**

Kellogg adapts the song "This Old Man" by showing a variety of dogs trying to get doggie treats from several old men. Readers are asked to count the number of dogs that appear throughout the book (250). Score and chords included. "This Old Man" can be found on the recording *Dana's Best Sing and Play-a-Long Tunes* by Dana (RMFK, 1995).

Kellogg, Steven. *Yankee Doodle.* **Simon & Schuster, 1996.**

Yankee Doodle is a young boy who accompanies his father to camp until a battle starts. He is almost captured by British soldiers but is rescued by his dog (the two run right off the illustration). He spends the rest of the war with his mother but helps celebrate the victory. The detailed illustrations will keep children amused for hours. Score included. The song can be found on the recording *Wee Sing America* by Pamela Beall and Susan Nipp (Price Stern Sloan, 1987).

Kovalski, Maryann. *Take Me Out to the Ballgame.* **Fitzhenry & Whiteside, 2004.**

Grandma takes Jenny and Joanna out of school for a trip to a baseball game. Once they are in sight of the stadium, they launch into the famous song and buy some "peanuts and Cracker Jacks" and "root, root, root for the home team." Score included. The song can be found on the recording *One Light One Sun* by Raffi (Troubadour, 1987).

Kovalski, Maryann. *The Wheels on the Bus*. Little, Brown, 1987.

Grandma takes Jenny and Joanna shopping for winter coats. They buy matching (and hilarious) large green coats. While waiting for the bus, Grandma leads them in song. They get so wrapped up in their song that they miss the bus and take a taxi home. Score included. The song can be found on the recording *Wiggleworms Love You* by the Old Town School of Folk Music (Old Town School, 2005).

Kubler, Annie. *Head, Shoulders, Knees, and Toes*. Child's Play, 2001.

This board book finds smiling babies pointing to the various parts of their bodies as they act out the song. They even have help from tiny stuffed animals. The final verse ends on the back cover. Score included. The song can be found on the recording *Music Is Magic* by the Magical Music Express (Magical Music Express, 2002). Other board books in Kubler's song series for Child's Play include

> *Baa, Baa, Black Sheep* (2005)
>
> *Down by the Station* (2005)
>
> *The Farmer in the Dell* (2001)
>
> *Here We Go round the Mulberry Bush* (2001)
>
> *If You're Happy and You Know It* (2001)
>
> *Incey Wincey Spider* (2005)
>
> *Ring around the Rosie* (2003)
>
> *Twinkle, Twinkle, Little Star* (2002)
>
> *Wheels on the Bus* (2003)

La Prise, Larry, Charles P. Macak, and Taftt Baker. *The Hokey Pokey*. Illustrated by Sheila Hamanaka. Simon & Schuster, 1997.

A young girl leads off the song by sticking her "red sneaker in." She's soon joined by a troupe of line dancers that grows into a huge cast of characters (including a few nonhuman dancers). Hamanaka's interesting perspectives make the book come alive. Score and chords included. The song can be found on several recordings, including *Family Dance* by Dan Zanes (Festival Five, 2001).

Langham, Tony. *Creepy Crawly Calypso.* **Illustrated by Debbie Harter. Barefoot Books, 2004.**

A group of tiny critters plays various instruments in this counting book. One spider plays steel drums, two butterflies play accordions, and so on through ten centipedes "tinkling pianos proudly." Score and chords included, along with a picture glossary of the creatures and the instruments.

Langstaff, John. *Frog Went A-Courtin'.* **Illustrated by Feodor Rojankovsky. Harcourt, 1955.**

Frog asks Mistress Mouse to marry him. Uncle Rat gives his consent, and all of the other animals help to make the wedding a big hit—that is, until a big cat sends them all scurrying. Score included. The song can be found on several recordings, including *Victor Vito* by Laurie Berkner (Two Tomatoes, 1999).

Lansky, Bruce. *Oh My Darling Porcupine and Other Silly Sing-Along Songs.* **Illustrated by Stephen Carpenter. Meadowbrook, 2006.**

Lansky and other poets have followed the Alan Katz model and created new lyrics to popular songs. "Tinkle, Tinkle, Little Cat" is sung, of course, to "Twinkle, Twinkle, Little Star." Children's artist Eric Ode has "Polly Ann from Tallahassee" to the tune of "Did You Ever See a Lassie?"

Lessac, Frane. *Camp Granada: Sing-Along Camp Songs.* **Holt, 2003.**

The lyrics and directions to more than thirty traditional camp favorites are featured along with Alan Sherman's "Hello Muddah, Hello Faddah" and Woody Guthrie's "This Land Is Your Land." Traditional songs include "Little Bunny Foo Foo," "Worms," and "Kum Ba Yah." Lessac's illustrations show the entire range of the camp experience, from boating and swimming to hiking and campfires.

Lewis, E. B. *This Little Light of Mine.* **Simon & Schuster, 2005.**

A young man is clearly feeling good about his life. He wanders around his small town waving to neighbors, helping an elderly woman pick up her scattered groceries, and inviting a lonely boy to join in a basketball game. Score and chords included. This oft-recorded song can be found on the recording *Rise and Shine* by Raffi (Troubadour, 1982).

Loesser, Frank. *I Love You! A Bushel and a Peck.* **Illustrated by Rosemary Wells. HarperCollins, 2005.**

Wells takes this hit from the Broadway musical *Guys and Dolls* and sets it in the country. A young farmer duck is distracted from tending his farm. He has trouble sleeping because of his love for a female duck that wears flowers in her hair. Score and chords included. The song "A Bushel and a Peck" can be found on the recording *Rocket Ship Beach* by Dan Zanes (Festival Five, 2000).

Long, Sylvia. *Hush Little Baby*. Chronicle, 1997.

The traditional lullaby promises the child many material objects. In this version, Long shows a mother pointing out many natural wonders, such as hummingbirds and shooting stars. Mama then reads the child a book and plays her banjo. The song can be found on the recording *Baby and Me* by Rachel Buchman (A Gentle Wind, 1991).

Mallet, David. *Inch by Inch: The Garden Song*. Illustrated by Ora Eitan. HarperCollins, 1995.

A child nurtures a garden, pulling weeds and "pickin' stones." Inch by inch, the child plants the seeds, battles crows, and dreams while waiting for the crops to grow. Score and chords included. The song "The Garden Song" can be found on the recording *Peter, Paul, and Mommy, Too* by Peter, Paul, and Mary (Warner Brothers, 1993).

Manning, Maurice J. *The Aunts Go Marching*. Boyds Mill, 2003.

The aunts go marching in the rain, under umbrellas, behind a young girl in a yellow rain outfit who is playing a drum. Thunder sends them scurrying back to their respective apartments. Astute readers will spot the young girl's own aunt and her dog in every double-page spread. The song "The Ants Go Marching" can be found on the recording *Camels, Cats, and Rainbows* by Paul Strausman (A Gentle Wind, 1982).

McCutcheon, John. *Happy Adoption Day!* Illustrated by Julie Paschkis. Little, Brown, 1996.

A man and a woman get their house ready for a new baby. We follow them as they fly across the ocean to get their child. Once back home, they are joined by other mixed-race families, and we get to watch the children grow older. Score included. The song can be found on the recording *Family Garden* by John McCutcheon (Rounder, 1993).

Merrill, Bob. *How Much Is That Doggie in the Window?* Illustrated by Iza Trapani. Gareth Stevens, 1999.

Trapani adds new verses to Merrill's song. A boy finds out that the puppy in the window of the pet shop costs sixty dollars. The boy only has eleven fifty. The pet shop owner tries to interest the boy in a hamster, gerbil, or mouse. The boy instead spends his money helping others and is rewarded with the dog. Score and chords included. The song can be found on the recording *Great Big Hits* by Sharon, Lois, and Bram (Elephant, 1992).

Milgrim, David. *Young MacDonald*. Dutton, 2006.

Young MacDonald creates weird hybrid animals on his farm. He combines a pig with a horse to create "a Hig." This new creature goes "With an oink-neigh here / And an oink-neigh there." He accidentally creates "a Bog," a boy and a dog, before setting things right. A version of "Old MacDonald" can be found on the recording *Wee Sing Animals, Animals, Animals* by Pamela Beall and Susan Nipp (Price Stern Sloan, 1999).

Mitchell, Joni. *Both Sides Now*. Illustrated by Alan Baker. Scholastic, 1992.

This story of two caterpillars changing into butterflies is paired with Mitchell's lyrics, especially the line "I've looked at life from both sides now." The song can be found on the recording *Clouds* by Joni Mitchell (Warner Brothers, 1967).

Mitchell, Joni. *Chelsea Morning*. Illustrated by Brian Froud. Milk and Cookies Press, 2004.

Several bizarre and beautiful imaginary characters greet a young girl in her bedroom. The girl herself appears as a robed character in the song's passage "And the sun poured in like butterscotch and stuck to all my senses." CD included.

Moore, Mary-Alice. *The Wheels on the School Bus*. Illustrated by Laura Huliska-Beith. HarperCollins, 2006.

The kids on the school bus say, "Off to school"; the teachers on the bus say, "Think, think, think"; the coach says, "Catch, catch, catch"; the nurse says, "Open wide"; the lunch ladies say, "Eat, eat, eat"; and—my favorite—the librarian on the bus says, "Read, read, read." The bus driver turns out to be the principal. Score and chords included. The traditional "Wheels on the Bus" can be found on the recording *Rise and Shine* by Raffi (Troubadour, 1982).

Nelson, Kadir. *He's Got the Whole World in His Hands*. Dial, 2005.

Family members in San Francisco are the focal point of this spiritual song. They are shown celebrating the sun and rain, moon and stars, rivers and mountains, brothers and sisters, and the whole world. Score and chords included. The song can be found on the recording *The Best of Gemini*, vol. 2, by Gemini (Gemini, 2005).

O'Brien, John. *The Farmer in the Dell.* **Boyds Mill, 2000.**

A farmer tumbles into a dell, a small ravine, and needs help getting out. It takes his wife, a nurse, a child, a dog, a cat, a rat, and a reluctant chunk of cheese to form a chain and pull him up. The song can be found on the recording *All-Time Children's Favorites* by the Learning Station (Monopoli/ Learning Station, 1993).

Ormerod, Jan. *If You're Happy and You Know It!* **Illustrated by Lindsey Gardiner. Star Bright, 2003.**

A little girl shows her happiness by clapping. A dog insists that waving your tail is a better way of showing your happiness. This is followed by an elephant flapping ears, a crocodile snapping teeth, and other animals. A version of the song can be found on the recording *Wide Wide World* by Miss Amy (Ionian, 2005).

Ormerod, Jan. *Ms. MacDonald Has a Class.* **Clarion, 1996.**

After Ms. MacDonald's class visits a farm, they decide to re-create the experience and put on a play. They plan, practice, build sets, and make costumes. The final play features cows, tractors, chickens, crows and scarecrows, sheep, pigs, bunnies, crops, and more. The traditional song can be found on the recording *Sing Along with Putumayo* (Putumayo, 2004).

Owen, Ann. *I've Been Working on the Railroad.* **Illustrated by Sandra D'Antonio. Picture Window Books, 2003.**

A banjo-playing train engineer heads over to Dinah's Place, where Dinah is blowing her horn. Score included. The song can be found on the recording *Come Ride Along with Me* by James Coffey (Blue Vision, 1997). Other books in the Traditional Songs series published by Picture Window Books include

> *The Ants Go Marching* (2004)
>
> *Clementine* (2004)
>
> *The Farmer in the Dell* (2004)
>
> *I Know an Old Lady Who Swallowed a Fly* (2004)
>
> *Old MacDonald Had a Farm* (2004)
>
> *She'll Be Coming around the Mountain* (2004)

Paley, Joan. *One More River: A Noah's Ark Counting Song.* **Little, Brown, 2002.**

Noah builds his ark, and the animals enter, starting with one elephant "chewing his honey bun." Other colorful featured animals include kangaroos, polar bears, bulls, llamas, monkeys, flamingos, aardvarks, turtles, and hens. Score included. The song can be found on the recording *One More River* by Bill Staines (Red House, 1998).

Paxton, Tom. *The Animals' Lullaby.* **Illustrated by Erick Ingraham. Morrow, 1993.**

Nature goes to sleep. We spot horses, otters, fish, and more heading for their resting spots. The final verse soothingly tells humans "Good night, children. Good night." Score and chords included.

Paxton, Tom. *Englebert the Elephant.* **Illustrated by Steven Kellogg. Morrow, 1990.**

Through some sort of oversight, Englebert the elephant is invited to the queen's ball. The court is shocked when Englebert does indeed show up. The queen regains control, and all are amazed when Englebert dances. The party eventually moves into the jungle. Paxton's version of the song can be found on his recording *Goin' to the Zoo* (Rounder, 1997).

Paxton, Tom. *Going to the Zoo.* **Illustrated by Karen Lee Schmidt. Morrow, 1996.**

Daddy takes the kids to visit the animals in the zoo. They watch the monkeys, bear, kangaroo, seals, lion, and birds before tiring out. Once back home, Daddy falls asleep on the couch, and the kids dance with their mother, singing, "Momma's takin' us to the zoo tomorrow!" Score and chords included. The song is on the recording *Goin' to the Zoo* by Tom Paxton (Rounder, 1997).

Paxton, Tom. *Jennifer's Rabbit.* **Illustrated by Donna Ayers. Morrow, 1988.**

Jennifer dreams of playing with her rabbit and a host of other animals throughout the night. They visit a zoo, dance through the forest, build a sand castle of moonbeams, and go sailing on a pirate ship. Paxton has the song on his recording *Goin' to the Zoo* (Rounder, 1997).

Paxton, Tom. *The Jungle Baseball Game.* **Illustrated by Karen Lee Schmidt. Morrow, 1999.**

The monkey baseball team is overconfident playing baseball against the hippo team. "Those slowpokes should just be glad / To get our autograph!" The hippos play harder and harder and win the game by catching a towering pop fly. Score and chords included.

Paxton, Tom. *The Marvelous Toy.* **Illustrated by Elizabeth Sayles. Morrow, 1996.**

A father brings home a strange toy that zips when it moves and bops when it stops and whirrs when it stands still. The boy plays with it and, years later, passes it on to his own son. Not until the final double-page illustration is the reader able to see the entire toy. Score and chords included. Paxton sings the song on the recording *Goin' to the Zoo* (Rounder, 1997).

Peek, Merle. *Roll Over: A Counting Song.* **Clarion, 1981.**

A boy is in bed with several animals. One by one, they fall off the bed and curl up on the floor, bench, bookcase, trunk, curtain rod, and chair. The final illustration shows the boy alone and asleep with the animals as part of the wallpaper border. Score and chords included. The song can be found on the recording *Get Ready, Get Set, Sing!* by Sarah Barchas (High Haven, 1994).

Pinkney, Brian. *Hush, Little Baby.* **Greenwillow, 2006.**

When the mother leaves, the father and the guitar-playing brother do their best to entertain a little girl. Papa brings the girl a mockingbird, a diamond ring, a looking glass, a spinning top, a dog, a horse and cart, and a fire truck. Mama returns to sing a lullaby. Score and chords included. A version of the song can be found on the recording *Jump Children* by Marcy Marxer (Rounder, 1997).

Prater, John. *The Bear Went over the Mountain.* **Barron's, 1999.**

This large board book features a bear cub climbing over a mountain. The mountain turns out to be a larger bear with pillows and blankets forming part of "the scenery." The song can be found on *Wee Sing Silly Songs* by Pamela Beall and Susan Nipp (Price Stern Sloan, 1982).

Priceman, Marjorie. *Froggie Went A-Courting.* **Little, Brown, 2000.**

Priceman adapts the traditional song about a frog who marries a mouse by setting it in New York City and adding new verses. The wedding party takes place "on top of the Statue of Liberty," and the wedding cake has as many layers as "floors in the Empire State." The song can be found on *You Are My Sunshine* by Elizabeth Mitchell (Last Affair, 2002).

Raffi. *Baby Beluga.* **Illustrated by Ashley Wolff. Crown, 1990.**

A little white whale frolics in the sea and interacts with its mother and several other aquatic creatures. Wolff's idyllic illustrations show polar bear, walrus, reindeer, puffin, and human child gathered together to celebrate the young whale. Score and chords included. The song can be found on the recording *Baby Beluga* by Raffi (Troubadour, 1980). Other Raffi picture books published by Crown/Knopf include

Down by the Bay (1987)

Everything Grows (1989)

Five Little Ducks (1989)

If You're Happy and You Know It (2005)

One Light, One Sun (1988)

Rise and Shine (1996)

Shake My Sillies Out (1987)

Spider on the Floor (1993)

This Little Light of Mine (2004)

Tingalayo (1988)

The Wheels on the Bus (1988)

Raschka, Chris. *Simple Gifts.* **Holt, 1998.**

Raschka shares this traditional Shaker hymn through abstract images that follow a cat and several woodland creatures. Score included. The song can be found on the recording *Red Grammer's Favorite Sing Along Songs* by Red Grammer (Red Note, 1993).

Rodgers, Richard, and Oscar Hammerstein. *Getting to Know You!* **Illustrated by Rosemary Wells. HarperCollins, 2002.**

Wells draws her anthropomorphic animals acting out the lyrics to several Rodgers and Hammerstein songs, including "Oh, What a Beautiful Morning," "Getting to Know You," "The Surrey with the Fringe on Top," "Oklahoma," "Some Enchanted Evening," and more. Scores included.

Rodgers, Richard, and Oscar Hammerstein. *My Favorite Things.* **Illustrated by Renée Graef. HarperCollins, 2001.**

This interpretation of the song from *The Sound of Music* shows a boy and girl and their family experiencing their favorite things through the course of a year. They smile at "raindrops on roses and whiskers on kittens" and play tea time in a playhouse with "bright copper kettles and warm woolen mittens." Score and chords included. The song can be found on *The Sound of Music* soundtrack (RCA, 1965).

Rogers, Sally. *Earthsong.* **Illustrated by Melissa Bay Mathis. Dutton, 1998.**

Grandpa and Grandma warn their grandchildren to share Mother Earth with several endangered species, including a panda, Bengal tiger, leatherback turtle, Indian python, American crocodile, and more. Score and chords included. "Over in the Endangered Meadow," which forms the book *Earthsong*, can be found on the recording *Piggyback Planet* by Sally Rogers (Round River, 1990).

Rose, Deborah Lee. *The Twelve Days of Kindergarten.* **Illustrated by Carey Armstrong-Ellis. Abrams, 2003.**

The kindergarten teacher gives her class "the whole alphabet from A to Z." She also gives them two picture books, three pencils, four puzzle shapes, five gold stars, six fish, seven stacks, eight beads, nine blocks, ten coins, eleven seeds, and "twelve eggs for hatching." "The Twelve Days of Christmas" can be found on the recording *A Very Merry Kidz Bop* by the Kidz Bop Kids (Razor & Tie, 2005). Rose has a sequel published by Abrams: *The Twelve Days of Winter* (2006).

Rounds, Glen. *I Know an Old Lady Who Swallowed a Fly.* **Holiday House, 1990.**

An old lady swallows a huge, scary-looking fly. The spider she swallows to catch the fly is even scarier. In fact, all of the animals and the old lady herself are frightening. The last scene is a tombstone. The song can be found on the recording *I Know an Old Lady* by Timmy Abell (Upstream, 1995).

Saport, Linda. *All the Pretty Little Horses.* **Clarion, 1999.**

A mother sings this traditional lullaby to her baby. The song inspires images of cakes, lambs, and several horses, "Blacks and bays, dapples and grays." Score and chords included. The lullaby can be found on the recording *Whaddaya Think of That?* by Laurie Berkner (Two Tomatoes, 2000).

Schwartz, Amy. *Old MacDonald.* **Scholastic, 1999.**

A young girl joins her family as they do their chores on the farm. A rooster wakes them up "with a cock-a-doodle here and a cock-a-doodle there." The book ends with a celebratory "And on this farm he had a song, E-I-E-I-O! With a tra la la here and a tra la la there . . ." Score and chords included. A traditional version of the song can be found on the recording *Sing Along with Bob #2* by Bob McGrath (Golden Books, 1990).

Scott, Michael. *Skidamarink! I Love You.* **Hyperion, 2004.**

Photographs of babies are featured with a Valentine's Day theme in this board book. The traditional song starts with the alliterative "Skidamarink a dink a dink, skidamarink a doo" and then expresses love in the morning, afternoon, and evening, "underneath the moon." The song titled "Skinnamarink" can be found on the recording *Great Big Hits 2* by Sharon, Lois, and Bram (Elephant, 2002).

Seeger, Laura Vaccaro. *I Had a Rooster.* **Viking, 2001.**

Seeger uses different layered pages to emphasize the cumulative effect of this traditional song. A boy interacts with a rooster, a cat, a duck, a cow, a pig, a sheep, a lion, and a baby—and they all make corresponding noises. Score and CD included.

Seeger, Pete. *One Grain of Sand: A Lullaby.* **Illustrated by Linda Wingerter. Little, Brown, 2002.**

Seeger wrote this lullaby for his own daughter. Wingerter shows double-page spreads of worldwide scenes, including island life, an underwater shot, an African savannah, ancient cities, wild horses, a nighttime city aerial view, and more. The last illustration shows a mother holding her two little ones. Score included. The song can be found on the recording *One Grain of Sand* by Odetta (Vanguard, 1963).

Seeger, Pete. *Turn! Turn! Turn!* Illustrated by Wendy Anderson Halperin. Simon & Schuster, 2003.

Illustrator Halperin utilizes a series of globes to feature the words that folksinger Seeger adapted from Ecclesiastes. Each globe shows multiple images related to the lyrics. Score and chords are included as well as a two-track CD featuring versions of the song by Seeger and the Byrds.

Sherman, Allan, and Lou Busch. *Hello Muddah, Hello Faddah! (A Letter from Camp)*. Illustrated by Jack E. Davis. Dutton, 2004.

A young boy writes to his parents about the horrors of summer camp. It constantly rains, the lake has alligators, and camp-mate Joe Spivy develops poison ivy. However, once the sun comes out, the young camper realizes how much fun he'll have and implores his parents to "kindly disregard this letter." The song can be found on the recording *Big Rock Rooster* by Daddy A Go Go (Boyd's Tone, 2002).

Slavin, Bill. *The Cat Came Back*. Albert Whitman, 1992.

Old Mister Johnson tries desperately to get rid of his cat. He sends it on an ocean liner, a hot-air balloon, and a train. The cat makes its way into the house, watching television with its seven kittens. A tornado finally carries the cat away (but it returns in a taxi). Score included. The song can be found on the recording *Fred's Favourites* by Fred Penner (Casablanca Kids, 2004).

Sloat, Teri. *There Was an Old Lady Who Swallowed a Trout*. Illustrated by Reynold Ruffins. Holt, 1998.

A lady swallows a trout, salmon, otter, seal, porpoise, walrus, whale, and the ocean. In the end, the creatures inside her make her hiccup and giggle, and they all swim out. The traditional song "I Know an Old Lady" can be found on the recording *Lollipops and Spaghetti* by "Miss Jackie" Silberg (Miss Jackie, 1979).

Smith, Will. *Just the Two of Us*. Illustrated by Kadir Nelson. Scholastic, 2001.

The book opens with Smith holding his baby in his arms and then watching his son grow before his eyes. The book ends with the reminder that "Daddy loves you for the rest of your life!" The song can be found on the recording *Big Willie Style* by Will Smith (Columbia, 1997).

Souhami, Jessica. *Old MacDonald.* **Orchard, 1996.**

Old MacDonald has a duck and a pig on his farm. The book then turns to a lift-the-flap format as Old MacDonald drives a sheep in a truck, a cow on a plane, and a Martian on a rocket ship. A lively version of the song can be found on the recording *We've All Got Stories* by the Dream Project (Rounder, 1996).

Spier, Peter. *The Star-Spangled Banner.* **Doubleday, 1973.**

Spier highlights Francis Scott Key's song by showing the American flag flying brightly through several battle scenes. The flag is then shown in a series of locations throughout the nation and even on the moon. Score and chords included. The song can be found on *Wee Sing America* by Pamela Beall and Susan Nipp (Price Stern Sloan, 1987).

Staines, Bill. *All God's Critters Got a Place in the Choir.* **Illustrated by Margot Zemach. Dutton, 1989.**

The bullfrogs, hippos, and cows sing the bass while "the dogs and cats they take up the middle." Zemach shows the many animals that make up the choir interspersed with illustrations of a family enjoying a fun day on their farm. Score included. The song can be found under the title "Place in the Choir" on the recording *The Happy Wanderer* by Bill Staines (Red House, 1993).

Sturges, Philomen. *She'll Be Comin' 'round the Mountain.* **Illustrated by Ashley Wolff. Little, Brown, 2004.**

Several creatures in America's Southwest eagerly await the arrival of an important visitor. New lyrics find the animals planning a fiesta and wondering "if she's a beauty or a bit too hooty-tooty." The readers finally learn that the new visitor is driving the "Six White Horses Book Mobile." A version of the song can be found on several recordings, including *Marvelous Day* by SteveSongs (Rounder, 2006).

Taback, Simms. *Joseph Had a Little Overcoat.* **Viking, 1999.**

Joseph's worn overcoat is remade into a jacket. From there, the material from the jacket is turned into a vest, a scarf, a necktie, a handkerchief, and a button. When the button is lost, Joseph makes a Caldecott Award–winning picture book out of nothing. Score and chords included. A similar song can be found under the title "I Had an Old Overcoat" by the Learning Station on the recording *Literacy in Motion* (Monopoli/Learning Station, 2005).

Taback, Simms. *There Was an Old Lady Who Swallowed a Fly.* **Viking, 1997.**

As the old lady swallows larger and larger animals, we can see through die-cut holes into her stomach. Taback does a humorous job of letting the reader know more about each animal through newspaper headlines, signage, and other aspects of collage artwork. This oft-recorded song can be found on the recording *Literacy in Motion* by the Learning Station (Monopoli/Learning Station, 2005).

Trapani, Iza. *Baa Baa Black Sheep*. Whispering Coyote, 2001.

The master, the dame, and the little boy leave the sheep's house with their wool. Afterward, different animals approach the sheep for other things. Instead, the sheep gives them all knitted items. A version of "Baa Baa Black Sheep" can be found on the recording *At the Bottom of the Sea* by Ralph's World (Mini Fresh, 2002). Other Whispering Coyote books by Trapani that feature new, extended versions of traditional songs include

> *Froggie Went A-Courtin'* (2002)
>
> *Here We Go round the Mulberry Bush* (2006)
>
> *I'm a Little Teapot* (1996)
>
> *The Itsy Bitsy Spider* (1993)
>
> *Jingle Bells* (2005)
>
> *Mary Had a Little Lamb* (1998)
>
> *Oh Where, Oh Where Has My Little Dog Gone?* (1995)
>
> *Row Row Row Your Boat* (1999)
>
> *Shoo Fly* (2000)
>
> *Twinkle, Twinkle, Little Star* (1994)

Ward, Jennifer. *Over in the Garden*. Illustrated by Kenneth J. Spengler. Rising Moon, 2002.

Mother insects and other tiny creatures teach their little ones. The praying mantis implores her youngster to pounce, while the mother ladybug tells her two little ones to crawl. Other characters include mosquitoes, snails, bees, spiders, butterflies, ants, and fireflies. Score and chords included. "Over in the Meadow," the song that inspired this book, can be found on the recording *Mail Myself to You* by John McCutcheon (Rounder, 1988).

Watson, Wendy. *Fox Went Out on a Chilly Night*. Lothrop, Lee & Shepard, 1994.

A fox supports his large family by stealing away into the night and grabbing a goose from a farm. Old Mother Slipper-Slopper raises the alarm, and John blows his horn and gives chase. The fox makes it back to his den, where "they never had such a feast in their life." Score included. The oft-recorded folk song "The Fox" can be found on the recording *Animal Songs* by Phil Rosenthal (American Melody, 1996).

Watson, Wendy. *Wendy Watson's Frog Went A-Courting.* Lothrop, Lee & Shepard, 1990.

Tiny detailed illustrations show a frog riding in a taxi pulled by a turtle to Miss Mousie's house, where he proposes to her. The wedding reception is interrupted by "an old bobcat," and "that was the end of the wedding day." The final illustration shows the frog and the mouse rowing away while some of the guests give treats to the smiling "bobcat." Score and chords included. A version of the song can be found on the recording *You Are My Sunshine* by Elizabeth Mitchell (Last Affair, 2002).

Weiss, George David, and Bob Thiele. *What a Wonderful World.* Illustrated by Ashley Bryan. Atheneum, 1995.

Louis Armstrong made this song a big hit and becomes a character in Bryan's depiction of a children's puppet show. Several multicultural children make puppet figures that represent themselves and the aspects of the world that the song celebrates. This beautiful song can be found on many recordings, including *Night Time* by Dan Zanes (Festival Five, 2002).

Welch, Willy. *Playing Right Field.* Illustrated by Marc Simont. Scholastic, 1995.

Nobody ever hits the baseball to right field, so the narrator has plenty of time to daydream. His thoughts are interrupted when he sees players yelling and pointing at him. Luckily, the ball falls into his glove. "Playing Right Field" can be found on the recording *Peter, Paul, and Mommy, Too* by Peter, Paul, and Mary (Warner Brothers, 1993).

Wells, Rosemary. *Bingo.* Scholastic, 1999.

Bingo features a black-and-white dog and is one of Wells's "Bunny Reads Back" series of lyrical board books. There are many recordings featuring "Bingo," including James Coffey's *Animal Groove* (Blue Vision, 1999). Other Wells books in this Scholastic series include

> *The Bear Went over the Mountain* (1998)
>
> *The Itsy-Bitsy Spider* (1998)
>
> *Old MacDonald* (1998)
>
> *Twinkle, Twinkle, Little Star* (2006)

Westcott, Nadine Bernard. *I Know an Old Lady Who Swallowed a Fly.* Little, Brown, 1980.

An old lady sets out refreshments for tea. A fly pops into her mouth. She gets the idea to swallow the fly, but that upsets her stomach. She next chases and swallows a bird, a cat, a dog, a goat, a cow, and a horse—but not before she terrorizes the countryside in hilarious two-page spreads. A version of the song can be found on the recording *I Know an Old Lady* by Timmy Abell (Upstream, 1995).

Westcott, Nadine Bernard. *Peanut Butter and Jelly.* **Dutton, 1987.**

A chef enters a house and helps a little boy and girl bake a gigantic loaf of bread. He saws a slice (with a saw) as a group of elephants joins them. The elephants crack and mash the peanuts to make peanut butter. They roll in a bathtub filled with grapes to make jelly. Everyone finally assembles a table-sized peanut butter and jelly sandwich. A hilarious version can be found on the recording *Music Is Magic* by Magical Music Express (Magical Music Express, 2002).

Westcott, Nadine Bernard. *Skip to My Lou.* **Little, Brown, 1989.**

While the farmer and his wife are gone, a boy dances with the cat. Things quickly get out of hand when the boy finds the cats in the buttermilk, the pigs in the parlor, the sheep in the bathtub—all dancing and making a mess of the place. Score and chords included. A version of "Skip to My Lou" can be found on the recording *Buzz Buzz* by Laurie Berkner (Two Tomatoes, 1998).

Whippo, Walt. *Little White Duck.* **Illustrated by Joan Paley. Music by Bernard Zaritsky. Little, Brown, 2000.**

A little mouse sings this song while strumming a guitar. The characters include a little white duck, a little green frog, a little black bug, and a little red snake. In the end, all of the characters take a bow on a stage. Score and chords included. The definitive recorded version can be found on *Burl Ives Sings Little White Duck* by Burl Ives (Columbia, 1974).

Winston, Jeannie. *Head, Shoulders, Knees, and Toes.* **Aladdin, 2003.**

A group of animals acts out the words to the songs, beginning with two frogs pointing to their heads. A monkey points to its shoulder while sitting on a giraffe, and the frogs return, pointing to their knees and toes, as does a ballerina hippo. A version of the song can be found on the recording *Here We Go Loopty Loo* by the Learning Station (Monopoli/Learning Station, 1998).

Zane, Alexander. *The Wheels on the Race Car.* **Illustrated by James Warhola. Orchard, 2005.**

Several animals drive their race cars "Round and Round" a race track. Their engines go "Vroom-Vroom-Vroom," the mechanics go "Zizz-Zizz-Zizz," and the checkered flag goes "Swish-Swish-Swish." The traditional version of "The Wheels on the Bus" can be found on the recording *Sing Along Stew* by Linda Arnold (Ariel, 1995).

Zanes, Dan. *Hello Hello.* **Illustrated by Donald Saaf. Little, Brown, 2004.**

A group of humans and anthropomorphic animals interacts in a city neighborhood. They are joined by anthropomorphic food, the sun, and clouds as they move into the countryside. A five-song CD is included as well as the score and chords for "Hello Hello" and the other songs.

Zanes, Dan. *Jump Up!* **Illustrated by Donald Saaf. Little, Brown, 2005.**

A cast of kids and anthropomorphic animals and objects (toaster, flowers, sun, animals, etc.) celebrates the day. They jump and dance and put on a concert in the countryside. A five-song CD is included as well as the score and chords for "Jump Up!" and the other songs.

Zelinsky, Paul O. *Knick-Knack Paddywhack.* **Dutton, 2002.**

Zelinsky has constructed an elaborate set of pull-tab, lift-the-flap, and other movable, paper-engineering tricks to illustrate the song "This Old Man." A boy, his dog, and a bone act out the story line, along with several tiny men. The song "This Old Man" can be found on the recording *Folk Playground* (Putumayo, 2006).

Zelinsky, Paul O. *The Wheels on the Bus.* **Dutton, 1990.**

Pull-tabs open and shut the bus doors and move the driver's arm, the windshield wipers, the mouths of the crying babies, and the shushing fingers of the mothers. The bus finally stops at the public library in time for a musical children's program. A version of the song can be found on the recording *Rise and Shine* by Raffi (Troubadour, 1982).

Ziefert, Harriet. *Sleepy-O!* **Illustrated by Laura Rader. Houghton Mifflin, 1997.**

Each family member tries a variety of ways to get the baby to stop crying, including playing musical instruments, rocking her, dancing with her, and giving her wagon rides. Sister finally realizes they are all too noisy for the baby to go to sleep. Score and chords included.

Ziefert, Harriet. *When I First Came to This Land.* **Illustrated by Simms Taback. Putnam, 1998.**

In 1885, an immigrant arrives in the United States and buys a farm. He quickly learns how tough it can be and names his farm "Muscle-in-My-Arm." A version of the song can be found on the recording *1, 2, 3, Four-Ever Friends* by Colleen and Uncle Squaty (Colleen and Uncle Squaty, 1995).

PICTURE BOOKS FEATURING MUSIC AND MUSICIANS

Ackerman, Karen. *Song and Dance Man*. Illustrated by Stephen Gammell. Knopf, 1988.

> Grandpa is excited when the kids come over to visit. He takes them upstairs to the attic and puts on a one-man vaudeville show. He dances, sings "Yankee Doodle," does magic tricks, tells jokes, and takes a bow. The kids love the show, and Grandpa tells them "he wouldn't trade a million good old days for the days he spends with us."

Aliki. *Ah, Music!* HarperCollins, 2003.

> Aliki gives a visual definition of music as sound, rhythm, melody, pitch and tone, volume, feeling, and creative art. She also includes a brief history of music and a look at the variety of music available. The overall theme of the book is "Music is for everyone!"

Auch, Mary Jane. *Bantam of the Opera*. Holiday House, 1997.

> Luigi the rooster sneaks aboard the farmer's truck and hides out at the opera house. When the tenor and his understudy come down with the chicken pox, the rooster saves the day with his perfect pitch.

Austin, Patricia. *The Cat Who Loved Mozart*. Illustrated by Henri Sorenson. Holiday House, 2001.

> Nine-year-old Jennifer finds a stray cat and names it Amadeus after her favorite composer, Wolfgang Amadeus Mozart. The cat shies away from Jennifer and even scratches her. Not until she practices the piano does Amadeus warm up to his new owner.

Battle-Levert, Gwendolyn. *The Music in Derrick's Heart*. Illustrated by Colin Bootman. Holiday House, 2000.

> Old Uncle Booker T teaches young Derrick how to play the harmonica. When old Arthur (another name for arthritis) comes to Uncle Booker T, Derrick brings him joy with his soulful harmonica playing.

Beall, Pamela, and Susan Nipp. *Wee Sing and Learn ABC*. Illustrated by Yudthana Pongmee. Price Stern Sloan, 2000.

> Various animals play different instruments; both animals and their instruments correspond to the letters of the alphabet, from "Abe the alligator plays the accordion" through "Zelda the zebra plays the zither." Other books in the Wee Sing and Learn series include

Wee Sing and Learn Colors (2000)

Wee Sing and Learn Dinosaurs (2001)

Wee Sing and Learn 123 (2000)

Bollinger, Max. *The Happy Troll.* **Illustrated by Peter Sis. Holt, 2005.**

Gus, a singing troll, is content to entertain the other trolls in exchange for food and simple objects. Gus becomes greedy and receives golden objects in exchange for his talent. Soon, he is all alone and must find his way back to his beautiful voice and forgotten songs.

Brett, Jan. *Berlioz the Bear.* **Putnam, 1991.**

On the way to a concert, a stubborn donkey sits in the middle of the road. Several animals come by to help, but they are unsuccessful. Finally, a bee flies out of Berlioz's bass, stings the donkey, and the musicians make it to the concert in time.

Bryant, Jen. *Music for the End of Time.* **Illustrated by Beth Peck. Eerdmans, 2005.**

Olivier Messiaen was given permission to compose music while held in a German prison during World War II. He was inspired by a nightingale to create his work "Quartet for the End of Time." When he played it for 5,000 prisoners in Stalag 8A, the music was "like birdsong, it was wild, beautiful, and full of hope."

Busse, Sarah Martin, and Jacqueline Briggs Martin. *Banjo Granny.* **Illustrated by Barry Root. Houghton Mifflin, 2006.**

Owen's granny packs up her banjo to visit her young grandson. She paddles the banjo case across a river, floats over a mountain with a balloon, and sails across a desert with her nightgown. When she arrives at Owen's house, "she strummed and sang her Owen-song from the first note to the last little trill."

Carle, Eric. *I See a Song.* **Scholastic, 1973.**

Brightly colored collage images represent the music that a musician plays. The violinist creates pictures of the moon, the sun, the ocean, flowers, and more. The musician is black and white when he first appears in the book and, by the end, becomes multicolored himself.

Carter, Don. *Heaven's All-Star Band.* **Knopf, 2002.**

A young boy imagines that Grandpa is in heaven listening to his beloved jazz. Famous jazz musicians playing for Grandpa include Louis Armstrong, Count Basie, John Coltrane, Miles Davis, Duke Ellington, Ella Fitzgerald, and more.

Cazet, Denys. *Dancing.* Orchard, 1995.

Alex is jealous of his new baby brother. His father spends time with him singing a song that asks "what's wrong?" "Go ahead and tell me, because . . . I love you. I love you." Alex and his father dance beneath the stars and moon, and Alex is reassured that he is still loved.

Cole, Barbara H. *Wash Day.* Illustrated by Ronald Himler. Star Bright Books, 2004.

While Miss Ett does the laundry, Grandpa entertains the children with his trumpet. They march around the clothes drying on the line singing and playing "Yankee Doodle." When Grandpa has a stroke, he encourages young Sherman to play.

Cowan, Catherine. *My Friend the Piano.* Illustrated by Kevin Hawkes. Lothrop, Lee & Shepard, 1998.

A little girl likes to compose on her piano, but her mother complains that she's only creating noise. The family decides to give the piano away to a woman who wants to turn it into a storage chest. The girl helps the piano escape into the sea.

Cox, Judy. *My Family Plays Music.* Illustrated by Elbrite Brown. Holiday House, 2003.

The young narrator proves that she is a percussionist by the time we meet the rest of her family. Her mother plays fiddle, her father plays cello, sister Emily plays clarinet in a marching band, and brother Paul plays lead guitar for a rock band.

Cronin, Doreen. *Dooby Dooby Moo.* Illustrated by Betsy Lewin. Atheneum, 2006.

The characters from the Click, Clack, Moo farm books are back and putting on a talent show in the barn. The cows sing "Twinkle, Twinkle, Little Star," the sheep sing "Home on the Range," and the pigs do an interpretive dance.

Curtis, Gavin. *The Bat Boy and His Violin.* Illustrated by E. B. Lewis. Simon & Schuster, 1998.

Reginald would rather play his violin than play baseball like his father, who is the manager of the Dukes, "the worst team in the Negro National League." Reginald becomes the team batboy and is able to play his violin in the dugout. His playing inspires the team to play better.

Cutler, Jane. *The Cello of Mr. O.* Illustrated by Greg Couch. Dutton, 1999.

The narrator and her family are refugees in a war-torn city. When Mr. O's cello is destroyed, the young narrator draws a picture of Mr. O playing the cello. He starts playing music again—this time with a harmonica—to keep hope alive.

Daly, Niki. *Ruby Sings the Blues*. Bloomsbury, 2005.

Ruby is sad because everyone always tells her to be quiet. A couple of neighbors who are jazz musicians teach Ruby to control her voice. Soon, everyone is exclaiming about Ruby's beautiful singing.

D'Arc, Karen Scourby. *My Grandmother Is a Singing Yaya*. Illustrated by Diane Palmisciano. Orchard, 2001.

Lulu is a little embarrassed by her Yaya's bursting into song at all occasions. Lulu does her best to keep Yaya too busy to sing at the school's Grandparent's Day picnic. In the end, the principal invites Yaya to lead the singing for the school's fiftieth anniversary.

Davol, Marguerite W. *The Loudest, Fastest, Best Drummer in Kansas*. Illustrated by Cat Bowman Smith. Orchard, 2000.

Maggie's constant drumming disrupts her town and causes the mayor to pass a law forbidding drumming. Maggie saves the day when a tornado strikes. She drums so fast and loud that "the tornado began to break apart, whirling itself to death in time with Maggie's drumbeat."

Demas, Corinne. *Nina's Waltz*. Illustrated by Deborah Lanino. Orchard, 2000.

Nina joins her father on a trip to a fiddle contest. Nina's father plans on playing his new composition, "Nina's Waltz." Unfortunately, he's stung on the hand by wasps. Nina competes instead and wins third prize.

Dodds, Dayle Ann. *Sing, Sophie!* Illustrated by Rosanne Litzinger. Candlewick, 1997.

Nobody appreciates little Sophie Adams's singing. Because of the singing, the baby won't nap, her sister's hair will fall flat, her brother can't catch any fish, and the cow won't give milk. When a thunderstorm scares Baby Jacob, Sophie's singing is the only thing that calms him down.

Elliot, David. *Hazel Nutt, Mad Scientist*. Illustrated by True Kelley. Holiday House, 2003.

Dr. Nutt enrages the local villagers when she creates a Frankensteinway—the Frankenstein monster in the shape of a piano. Instead of storming her lab, the villagers are entertained by her monster. "The crowd's favorite number is 'Old MacDonald Had a Bat.'"

Elya, Susan Middleton. *Sophie's Trophy*. Illustrated by Viviana Garofoli. Putnam, 2006.

Sophie the frog feels inferior to her talented brother in this bilingual picture book. She learns that her special talent is singing. She earns her own trophy—*trofeo*—at a bog talent show.

Falconer, Ian. *Olivia Forms a Band*. Atheneum, 2006.

Olivia becomes a one-person band. After making a racket with her xylophone-drum-bell-pot lids-whistle outfit, she quickly loses interest and decides to put on some makeup instead. The shots of Olivia smiling with lipstick on are priceless.

Fleming, Candace. *Gabriella's Song*. Illustrated by Giselle Potter. Atheneum, 1997.

Gabriella hears "her mother's voice mingled with the city's sounds" and makes a song. The song passes from a baker to a widow to a gondolier. A composer hears Gabriella's song and turns it into a symphony.

George-Warren, Holly. *Honky-Tonk Heroes and Hillbilly Angels: The Pioneers of Country and Western Music*. Illustrated by Laura Levine. Houghton Mifflin, 2006.

Several country musicians are profiled in two-page sketches, including Hank Williams, Johnny Cash, Patsy Cline, Loretta Lynn, the Carter Family, Gene Autry, and the Father of Bluegrass Music—Bill Monroe.

Gerstein, Mordicai. *What Charlie Heard*. Farrar, Straus and Giroux, 2002.

Charlie Ives grew up listening to all of the sounds around him, such as the church bell and thunderstorms. Charlie and his musical father always tried to capture these sounds. Not until Charlie was an old man did the world finally hear his compositions.

Gibbons, Faye. *Emma Jo's Song*. Illustrated by Sherry Meidell. Boyds Mills, 2001.

The entire Puckett family is musical except for Emma Joy, who is shy about singing. She starts singing "This Little Light of Mine" at a family reunion and is joined by her howling dog Rip. The entire clan sings along, and Grandpa acknowledges "that girl's got a gift."

Gilmor, Don. *The Fabulous Song*. Illustrated by Marie-Louise Gay. Kane/Miller, 1998.

Little Frederic's parents expect him to be a great musician. As he grows older, Frederic tries "almost every instrument in the orchestra." In the end, he finds his true role as a conductor, bringing order to his own household of musicians.

Gollub, Matthew. *The Jazz Fly*. Illustrated by Karen Hanke. Tortuga Press, 2000.

A drum-playing fly meets several animals that give him directions to a club. The fly's band is eventually threatened to come up with a new sound. The Jazz Fly incorporates the various animal sounds he heard into his drumming.

Goss, Linda. *The Frog Who Wanted to Be a Singer.* Illustrated by Cynthia Jabar. Orchard, 1996.

A talented frog decides to leave his lily pad and sing for others. He meets a lot of resistance and suffers stage fright. He overcomes his fears, sings in boogie-woogie style, and gets everyone up dancing. Apparently, "that is how Rhythm and Blues was born."

Gray, Libba Moore. *When Uncle Took the Fiddle.* Illustrated by Lloyd Bloom. Orchard, 1999.

Everyone's tired until Uncle plays his fiddle. Grandma fetches her mouth harp, Mama plays the guitar, Papa plays the washboard, and the kids play percussion. Neighbors hear the music and join in with their own instruments. Everyone dances into the wee hours.

Griffith, Helen V. *Georgia Music.* Illustrated by James Stevenson. Greenwillow, 1986.

A girl spends the summer with her grandfather. They both enjoy listening to the summer country sounds. Grandfather captures those sounds in his tunes on the mouth organ. The girl eventually re-creates the country sounds with her own playing.

Harper, Wilhelmina. *The Gunniwolf.* Illustrated by Barbara Upton. Dutton, 2003.

A little singing girl goes deeper and deeper into the jungle to pick flowers. The Gunniwolf tells the girl to sing her song again, and when she does, the creature falls asleep. The girl runs away but is caught by the Gunniwolf. They repeat the process until the girl arrives safely at home.

Hoff, Syd. *Arturo's Baton.* Clarion, 1996.

Arturo, the conductor, is convinced that his baton is the reason why he is so successful. When the baton goes missing, Arturo is upset and wants to cancel his tour. He learns that he is a great conductor even without his baton.

Horowitz, Dave. *Soon Baboon Soon.* Putnam, 2005.

Several types of primates give a percussion concert. Baboon patiently waits to play while the chimps play timpani, the gorilla plays the gong, and the monkeys play the trap set. Finally, Baboon plays "Ting" on his triangle to thunderous applause.

Howe, James. *Horace and Morris Join the Chorus (but What about Dolores?).* Illustrated by Amy Walrod. Atheneum, 2002.

Dolores has a voice that "no one had ever heard before." She doesn't make the school chorus even though her friends Horace and Morris did. She's sad until her music teacher realizes her songwriting ability.

Hyde, Judith Jensen. *Rainy-Day Music.* **Illustrated by Jason Abbott. Scholastic, 2006.**

A young boy is sad because he's stuck indoors on a rainy day. His father shows him how to make musical instruments out of glasses filled with various amounts of water in them. "Some call it a ghost fiddle. That's my favorite name," exclaims the boy's dad.

Igus, Toyomi. *I See the Rhythm.* **Illustrated by Michele Wood. Children's Book Press, 1998.**

African American music is expressed through art, poetic text, and time lines from the music of Africa through slave songs, blues, ragtime, jazz, gospel, rhythm and blues, soul music, rock and roll, funk, rap, and hip-hop.

Isadora, Rachel. *Ben's Trumpet.* **Greenwillow, 1979.**

Young Ben admires the jazz musicians who play at a nearby club. Ben plays an imaginary trumpet but stops when the other kids make fun of him. Finally, the trumpet player from the club recognizes a future musician in Ben and gives him a lesson on a real trumpet.

Isadora, Rachel. *Bring On That Beat.* **Putnam, 2002.**

Black-and-white illustrations of Harlem in the 1930s are highlighted by colorful images that bring out the flavor of jazz music. Young rappers of today are reminded that "When cats played the beat / It was jazz on the street."

Jackson, Chris. *The Gaggle Sisters River Tour.* **Lobster Press, 2002.**

The Gaggle Sisters float on a river and search for an audience. Sadie sings and Dorothy plays the accordion (and does all the work). Sadie decides to sing "Listen Up, Moon," and they create a canvas backdrop featuring the moon and its reflection. Jackson's sequel, published by Lobster Press, is titled *The Gaggle Sisters Sing Again* (2003).

James, Simon. *Baby Brains, Superstar.* **Candlewick, 2005.**

The smartest baby in the world becomes a big sensation with his skills on the electric guitar. But when he finds himself onstage in an outdoor stadium facing an enormous crowd, he panics and cries. His live recording of "I Want My Mommy" becomes a huge worldwide hit.

Jewell, Nancy. *Sailor Song.* **Illustrated by Stefano Vitale. Clarion, 1999.**

A mother sings a lullaby about the sea and a sailor returning home. Images show the boat floating over the beach, through the woods, over a pond, up a hill, across a field, and finally up the stairs of the bedroom.

Johnson, Angela. *Violet's Music.* Illustrated by Laura Huliska-Beith. Dial, 2004.

Violet knew she was a musician when she was just a baby a few hours old banging her rattle. As she grew older, she looked for other musicians her age. One day, while playing her guitar in the park, she finds a girl beating a drum, a boy playing a saxophone, and a singer.

Ketcham, Sallie. *Bach's Big Adventure.* Illustrated by Timothy Bush. Orchard, 1999.

This fictionalized account of young Johann Sebastian Bach tells of his desire to be the best organist in all of Germany. He is devastated when he hears his rival, old Adam Reincken, playing. However, Reincken listens to Bach play and tells him, "I thought the art had died, but now I see it lives in you."

Kitamura, Satoshi. *Igor: The Bird Who Couldn't Sing.* Farrar, Straus and Giroux, 2005.

A crow loves to sing, but he has an awful voice that causes the other birds to fall out of the trees laughing. Feeling sad, he flies to an isolated place where he can sing and no one can hear him. Igor finds a long-lost Dodo, who thinks the crow's singing is delightful.

Krosoczka, Jarrett J. *Punk Farm.* Knopf, 2005.

A barnyard rock band features a sheep singing lead vocals. A goat plays the bass guitar, a pig plays lead guitar, a chicken plucks the keyboards, and a cow bangs away at the drums. The band sings their hit song to the tune of "Old MacDonald Had a Farm" and ends with a rousing "Thank you Wisconsin!"

Kushner, Tony. *Brundibar.* Illustrated by Maurice Sendak. Hyperion, 2003.

Two children rush to town to buy fresh milk for their sick mother. No one will give them milk without money. They see a hurdy-gurdy man named Brundibar making money, and they decide to sing themselves. Unfortunately, Brundibar scares them away. Three hundred children come to the rescue.

Kuskin, Karla. *The Philharmonic Gets Dressed.* Illustrated by Marc Simont. HarperCollins, 1982.

One hundred and five people get ready for work. One hundred and four people are onstage with their instruments. They play beautiful music for hundreds of people under the direction of one conductor.

Lithgow, John. *The Remarkable Farkle McBride.* Illustrated by C. F. Payne. Simon & Schuster, 2000.

Child prodigy Farkle masters the violin at the age of three but eventually grows tired of it. As he grows up, he goes through a series of musical instruments in a similar manner. At the age of ten, he discovers his true passion—leading an orchestra as the conductor.

London, Jonathan. *Froggy Plays in the Band.* Illustrated by Frank Remkiewicz. Viking, 2000.

Froggy and his friends start a marching band. Despite an accident that has them crashing into each other, the band wins a special award. Froggy earns an embarrassing kiss from Frogilina, the baton twirler.

London, Jonathan. *Hip Cat.* Illustrated by Woodleigh Hubbard. Chronicle, 1993.

A saxophone-playing cat leaves his shack by the river and heads for the city. He plays jazz for the other cats, but all of the best-paying joints are owned by the dogs. Eventually, he becomes a famous musician and becomes known as "one cool daddy-o."

Macken, JoAnn Early. *Sing-Along Song.* Illustrated by LeUyen Pham. Viking, 2004.

A young boy enjoys singing throughout his day. He greets a robin in the morning and sings along: "Cheery day! Mornin', sun!" He also sings like a bee: "Busy buzz, dizzy fuzz!" He does the same thing with a squirrel and his dog, cat, father, and baby sister.

Madison, Alan. *Pecorino's First Concert.* Illustrated by AnnLaura Cantone. Atheneum, 2005.

Pecorino attends a concert directed by the world famous Pimplelini. Pecorino somehow manages to get stuck inside a tuba. The tuba player blows hard enough to send Pecorino flying through the air, right into his mother's arms.

McCloskey, Robert. *Lentil.* Viking, 1940.

Lentil is an expert harmonica player. When a dignitary arrives in town, mean Old Sneep sucks on a lemon loud enough to make the musician's lips pucker too much to play. Lentil saves the day by playing "Comin' 'round the Mountain When She Comes."

McKenzie, Tim. *Baxter Barret Brown's Bass Fiddle.* Illustrated by Charles Shaw. Bright Sky Press, 2004.

Baxter transforms his bass fiddle into a bass fiddle bicycle and takes it down the road. When he comes upon a lake, he turns it into a bass fiddle boat. He next transforms it into a bass fiddle house but misses making music with it.

Miller, William. *The Piano*. Illustrated by Susan Keeter. Lee and Low, 2000.

A young African American girl and her elderly white employer develop a friendship over their love of music. Miss Hartwell, whose own hands hurt too much to play much anymore, gives Tia piano lessons. Tia, in turn, teaches Miss Hartwell a way to relieve the pain in her hands.

Miller, William. *Rent Party Jazz*. Illustrated by Charlotte Riley-Webb. Lee and Low, 2001.

Sonny is worried because his mother lost her job and is unable to pay the rent. Smilin' Jack, a street musician, promises to help out by throwing a rent party. Folks come by for good music and dancing and toss coins in a bucket.

Millman, Isaac. *Moses Goes to a Concert*. Farrar, Straus and Giroux, 1998.

Moses is a deaf boy who loves to play the drums. He and his classmates, who are also deaf, attend a young people's concert. They are inspired by a deaf musician who plays an array of percussion instruments.

Moss, Lloyd. *Music Is*. Illustrated by Philippe Petit-Roulet. Putnam, 2003.

A boy hears all kinds of music throughout an entire day. Moss has written a tribute to how music enhances everyone's lives. "Music fills our lives with magic; music is a wondrous thing."

Moss, Lloyd. *Our Marching Band*. Illustrated by Diana Cain Bluthenthal. Putnam, 2001.

Several children form a marching band but produce a noise that stuns the neighborhood. The kids devote themselves to practice and are soon invited to march in the big Fourth of July parade.

Moss, Lloyd. *Zin! Zin! Zin! A Violin*. Illustrated by Marjorie Priceman. Simon & Schuster, 1995.

A lone trombone player plays onstage. He is joined by a trumpet player, and they become a duo. Other musicians enter and play. They become an orchestra led by a conductor and playing before an appreciative audience (which includes two cats, a dog, and a mouse).

Myers, Walter Dean. *Blues Journey*. Illustrated by Christopher Myers. Holiday House, 2003.

The reader is introduced to "a truly American music, the Blues" through a series of blues-styled poems. The songs reflect specific incidents in African American history as well as universal emotions. This multiple-award-winning book is in picture-book format but best suited for upper-elementary through high school.

Myers, Walter Dean. *The Blues of Flats Brown.* **Illustrated by Nina Laden. Holiday House, 2000.**

Flats is a junkyard dog that loves to play the blues on his guitar. He escapes his cruel owner and becomes a hit musician, writing songs like "The Junkyard Heap." A. J. Grubbs, Flats's owner, follows Flats to New York but is touched when he hears Flats play "The Gritty Grubbs Blues."

Myers, Walter Dean. *Jazz.* **Illustrated by Christopher Myers. Holiday House, 2006.**

This father-and-son team shows different aspects of jazz music through a series of poems. Titles include "Twenty-Finger Jack," "Be-Bop," "Jazz Vocal," "Three Voices," and "Louie, Louie, How You Play So Sweet?"

Nygaard, Elizabeth. *Snake Alley Band.* **Illustrated by Betsy Lewin. Doubleday, 1998.**

A young snake grows tired of his snake band. He seeks out the animals he dismissed earlier—a cricket with its "Chew-up," a frog croaking "Cha-bop," a fish bubbling "Pop-pop-doo-wop," a bird singing "Tweet-tweedle-dee-deet," and a turtle thumping "Ta-toom."

Panahi, H. L. *BeBop Express.* **Illustrated by Steve Johnson and Lou Fancher. Amistad, 2005.**

A special train fills up with passengers and takes a musical journey. It leaves New York and stops in Philadelphia, Chicago, and St. Louis, picking up a new jazz musician at each stop. The final stop is New Orleans for a "traffic-jam jammin' show out in the street."

Parish, Herman. *Bravo, Amelia Bedelia!* **Illustrated by Lynn Sweat. Greenwillow, 1997.**

Amelia Bedelia was sent to pick up the conductor, but he was too heavy. She tries to play the violin by ear (she rubs her ear across the strings). She looks for wind instruments and comes back with electric fans. Still, she inspires young children to join the orchestra.

Pearson, Deborah. *Big City Song.* **Illustrated by Lynn Rowe Reed. Holiday House, 2006.**

The big city noises make musical sounds. Vehicles rushing by go "Dwop-dwop-dwop-dwop-whizzzzzzz. Yip! Yip! BLAAAAAP!" Church bells play slow, sad songs. Park trees shake a leafy hula dance. The nighttime brings its own city sounds when creatures bang rhythms on garbage-can lids.

Pellekaan, Karen van Holst. *Coco Makes Music*. Illustrated by Vera de Backker. Gareth Stevens, 2000.

Coco the koala and Wally the kangaroo make music on a variety of instruments they make from nature. They blow into a hollow stick, make shakers out of poppy-seed pods and bean pods, create a rattle out of pebbles, and more. When a thunderstorm forces them into a cave, they give their instruments to other animals and have a concert.

Perkins, Lynne Rae. *Snow Music*. Greenwillow, 2003.

Natural sounds can be interpreted as musical sounds. "Snow came singing a silent song." A dog runs out of the house, and his huffing and collar bell make music. A passing car and truck have their own songs. We see that the action takes place in a snow globe.

Pinkney, Andrea Davis. *Duke Ellington*. Illustrated by Brian Pinkney. Hyperion, 1998.

This picture-book biography follows Duke Ellington from his childhood through to his Carnegie Hall appearance in 1943. Brian Pinkney's scratch-board illustrations show the music flying out of the radio and the musical instruments of Ellington's band members.

Pinkney, Andrea Davis. *Ella Fitzgerald: The Tale of a Vocal Virtuosa*. Illustrated by Brian Pinkney. Hyperion, 2002.

Scat Cat Malone tells Ella Fitzgerald's story from her childhood in Yonkers, New York, to singing to a sold-out concert in Carnegie Hall. Ella highlighted a famous battle of the bands, cowrote the song "A-Tisket, A-Tasket," and was also known as the Queen of Scat.

Pinkney, Brian. *Max Found Two Sticks*. Simon & Schuster, 1994.

One windy day, two sticks fall down, and Max starts tapping them on his thighs. Next, he starts beating the sticks on a bucket to imitate rain. He moves on to clanging soda bottles and then garbage cans. A marching band goes down the street, and the last drummer tosses Max his spare sticks.

Price, Kathy. *The Bourbon Street Musicians*. Illustrated by Andrew Glass. Clarion, 2002.

This retelling of the Bremen Town Musicians finds a musical horse, hound dog, rooster, and cat heading to New Orleans. They find a group of ruffians eating a huge meal in a shack. The animals sing in hopes of getting an invitation to eat but instead scare the thieves.

Raschka, Chris. *Charlie Parker Played Be Bop.* **Orchard, 1992.**

Raschka captures the sounds of jazz saxophone player Charlie Parker's music through both the art and the rhythm of the text. "Be bop. Fisk, fisk. Lollipop. Boomba, boomba. . . . Never leave your cat alone."

Raschka, Chris. *John Coltrane's Giant Step.* **Atheneum, 2002.**

John Coltrane's musical composition "A Giant Step" is performed by a box, a snowflake, and a kitten. The narrator gives proper instructions to the performers, and they complete the performance by faithfully following Coltrane's special musical attributes.

Rockwell, Anne. *Root-a-Toot-Toot.* **Macmillan, 1991.**

A little boy plays "Root-a-Toot-Toot" on his little flute in this cumulative rebus story. Along the way, the boy meets up with a variety of noisy animals. They journey further until they meet a farmer and his wife and head back home.

Rylant, Cynthia. *Mr. Putter and Tabby Toot the Horn.* **Illustrated by Arthur Howard. Harcourt, 1998.**

Mr. Putter and his neighbor Mrs. Teaberry decide to learn to play instruments. Mr. Putter tries to play a horn but fails. Mrs. Teaberry learns to play the mandolin. She winds up not only entertaining the two of them and their pets but feeding them, as well.

Schaap, Martine, and Alex de Wolf. *Mop's Backyard Concert.* **Cricket, 2001.**

Mop the dog gets away from his family in the park. They find him singing along with a band. The family is inspired to create homemade instruments, and they have a concert in the backyard—with Mop howling along.

Seeger, Pete. *Abiyoyo.* **Illustrated by Michael Hays. Macmillan, 1986.**

A magician and his son battle the monster Abiyoyo. The boy strums his ukulele and sings to the monster "A-BI-YO-YO, BI-YO-YO, YO-YO-YO." The monster starts dancing. When he falls down from exhaustion, the magician zaps him with his wand, and Abiyoyo disappears.

Shannon, George. *Lizard's Song.* **Illustrated by Jose Aruego and Ariane Dewey. Greenwillow, 1981.**

Lizard sings a song about living on his rock. Bear learns the song but forgets it whenever he's interrupted by other animals. Lizard convinces Bear to come up with his own personal song about living in a den.

Steig, William. *Roland the Minstrel Pig.* HarperCollins, 1968.

Roland becomes a wandering minstrel in search of an audience. He meets up with a tricky fox that plans to eat Roland. Roland is saved by the lion king and becomes a famous musician.

Stenmark, Victoria. *The Singing Chick.* Illustrated by Randy Cecil. Holt, 1999.

A fox swallows a singing chick and begins to sing himself. He is swallowed by a wolf that is, in turn, swallowed by a bear. The bear rolls down a hill, into a tree, and out pop the other animals. The bigger animals return the chick to "his mother, the singing hen."

Taylor, Debbie A. *Sweet Music in Harlem.* Illustrated by Frank Morrison. Lee and Low, 2004.

A photographer is coming to take a picture of Uncle Click, a jazz musician, but his trademark hat is missing. C. J. hunts for it throughout the neighborhood, telling everyone about the photographer coming. In the end, several musicians show up for the picture.

Thaler, Mike. *The Music Teacher from the Black Lagoon.* Illustrated by Jared Lee. Scholastic, 2000.

A boy is worried about his music teacher's reputation. Reportedly, she wears armor, breaks children's glasses by hitting a high C, makes you sing in front of girls and memorize a zillion notes, and zaps you with her laser baton if you miss one note. Of course, he finds out that his music teacher is really cool.

Velasquez, Eric. *Grandma's Records.* Walker, 2001.

Young Eric spends his summers with his grandmother and learns about her favorite music. They are invited to Puerto Rico's best band's first concert in New York. The lead singer dedicates the final song—"En mi viejo San Juan/In My Old San Juan"—to Grandma.

Walter, Mildred Pitts. *Ty's One-Man Band.* Illustrated by Margot Tomes. Scholastic, 1980.

Ty heads down to a pond and hears strange, rhythmic sounds. He spots a mysterious man who juggles his plates after eating his meal. The man introduces himself as a one-man band. He creates music from everyday objects, such as wooden spoons, pails, and combs.

Weatherford, Carole Boston. *Jazz Baby.* Illustrated by Laura Freeman. Lee and Low, 2002.

Several children sing, dance, and play a variety of instruments to a jazz-influenced text. "Jazz baby, jazz baby, blow your horn. You've got rhythm sure as you're born." The kids are worn out by the end of the book and collapse on the floor with smiles on their faces.

Weaver, Tess. *Opera Cat.* **Illustrated by Andréa Wesson. Clarion, 2002.**

When Madame SoSo gets laryngitis, her cat Alma's secret comes out. Alma had been secretly practicing opera. Alma hides under Madame SoSo's costume and sings the night of the big premiere. During the final bow, Madame SoSo rewards Alma by lifting the cat up for all to see.

Webb, Steve. *Tanka Tanka Skunk!* **Orchard, 2003.**

Tanka, an elephant, and Skunk beat out the rhythms of several animal names on their drums. "Cat-er-pil-lar Big Gorilla Yakety Yakety Yak." At the end of the cacophonous text, the narrator encourages the reader "Once more from the top . . . faster this time, please!"

Wells, Rosemary. *Practice Makes Perfect.* **Illustrated by Jody Wheeler. Hyperion, 2002.**

Timothy plays his coffee cans in hopes of having a solo in the class talent show. His teacher convinces him to play the bells. Timothy's classmate Yoko teaches him how to read music, and he plays his solo perfectly.

Williams, Vera B. *Lucky Song.* **Greenwillow, 1997.**

After a busy day of flying a kite, little Evie's father comes into her bedroom and sings her a song about her day. The text ends with the narrator inviting the reader to go to the beginning of the book to hear Evie's song again.

Williams, Vera B. *Something Special for Me.* **Greenwillow, 1983.**

Mama decides to let Rosa buy her own birthday gift from the money in the big jar. Rosie almost buys skates, a new outfit, and camping gear, but these items are "not the special presents I wanted to empty the big jar for." Rosa hears a man play an accordion and decides that music is the best present.

Winter, Jeanette. *Follow the Drinking Gourd.* **Knopf, 1988.**

Runaway slaves learned a song that helped them make their way to freedom. "For the old man is a-waiting for you to carry you to freedom / If you follow the drinking gourd." The gourd stands for the Big Dipper constellation, which points to the North Star and the direction to Canada.

Winter, Jonah. *Once Upon a Time in Chicago: The Story of Benny Goodman.* **Illustrated by Jeanette Winter. Hyperion, 2000.**

Benny Goodman grew up in a poor neighborhood in Chicago. As a young boy, he quickly grew proficient playing the clarinet. When his father died, Benny expressed his emotions through his clarinet "until everyone in the world had heard his beautiful music."

Winter, Jonah. *The 39 Apartments of Ludwig van Beethoven*. Schwartz & Wade, 2006.

Beethoven lived in no fewer than thirty-nine apartments throughout Vienna. He also owned several legless pianos. The author develops hilarious theories why Beethoven had to move so often and how these pianos were moved from one apartment to another.

Zion, Gene. *Harry and the Lady Next Door*. Illustrated by Margaret Bloy Graham. HarperCollins, 1960.

The lady next door sings so loudly and so badly that she hurts Harry the dog's ears. Her singing is louder than the fire-truck's sirens, and she even makes the cats run away. Harry helps her win a local talent contest, where she is awarded the prize of studying "music in a far-off country for a long time!"

PICTURE BOOKS FEATURING DANCE AND DANCERS

Allen, Debbie. *Dancing in the Wings*. Illustrated by Kadir Nelson. Dial, 2000.

Celebrity dancer-choreographer Allen tells the story of Sassy, a girl with large feet and long legs. Sassy dreams of being a ballerina and fights the ridicule of others. She eventually wins the audition to take part in a summer dance festival in Washington, D.C.

Andreae, Giles. *Giraffes Can't Dance*. Illustrated by Guy Parker-Rees. Orchard, 2001.

Every year, the animals in Africa perform at the Jungle Dance. They ridicule Gerald the giraffe because he dances poorly. A cricket helps Gerald listen to the music in nature and the moon and become a strong dancer.

Appelt, Kathi. *The Alley Cat's Meow*. Illustrated by Jon Goodell. Harcourt, 2002.

A fancy cat named Red meets Miss Ginger in a boogie-woogie joint called the Alley Cat's Meow. They jitterbug, waltz, samba, and "cat-trot." They go on to dance on Broadway and on the silver screen.

Appelt, Kathi. *Piggies in a Polka*. Illustrated by LeUyen Pham. Harcourt, 2003.

Pigs arrive at a farm for the annual hootenanny. There's even a sign that tells them to "Do the Hokey Porky Tonight!" We meet the musicians and the singer Porcina. The pigs dance up a storm, even forming a piggy mosh pit.

Appelt, Kathi. *Rain Dance*. Illustrated by Emilie Chollat. HarperCollins, 2001.

When the rain falls, different animals move in different ways. This simple counting book features a frog, spiders, chicks, calves, pigs, rabbits, ducklings, puppies, and kittens before ending with ten ponies prancing in a rain dance.

Appelt, Kathi. *Toddler Two-Step.* Illustrated by Ward Schumaker. HarperCollins, 2000.

Several toddlers spin and dance to a counting ditty. "Seven, eight, clap, clap, clap / Toes out straight, tappity-tap." The song then counts back down to two and one. "Now we've done / The toddler two-step."

Arnold, Marsha Diane. *Prancing Dancing Lily.* Illustrated by John Manders. Dial, 2004.

Lily the cow flops at square dancing, kicking up her legs with the Rockettes, and tap dancing on a cruise ship. However, she has fun joining a conga line and rushes home to teach the other cows to prance and dance.

Asch, Frank. *Moondance.* Scholastic, 1993.

Bear thinks he is dancing with the clouds when fog appears. Then he dances with the rain. He asks the moon to dance with him and succeeds when he sees the moon's reflection in a puddle.

Auch, Mary Jane. *Hen Lake.* Holiday House, 1995.

Poulette the hen dreams of being a ballerina. She is ridiculed by the vain new peacock. Poulette encourages the other chickens to dance with her in a performance of *Hen Lake.* The hens and the peacock join talents for the final number.

Beaumont, Karen. *Baby Danced the Polka.* Illustrated by Jennifer Plecas. Dial, 2004.

Baby refuses to go to bed. Instead, Baby dances the polka with a polka-dotted pig, a little goat, a cow, and a shaggy sheep in this lift-the-flap picture book. The baby's parents join him in "the best ol' polka-fest in all of Arkansas!"

Bottner, Barbara. *Bootsie Barker Ballerina.* Illustrated by G. Brian Karas. HarperCollins, 1997.

Bootsie bullies the other dancers in dance lessons. She constantly picks on Bernie, exclaiming, "I hate boys." Bootsie is eventually tricked into dancing like a tornado, and she spins out the door.

Bradley, Kimberly Brubaker. *Ballerino Nate.* Illustrated by R. W. Alley. Dial, 2006.

Ben is constantly telling his brother, Nate, that boys can't be ballerinas. Nate turns out to be the only boy in his ballet class. It's not until he attends a professional ballet show and meets a male dancer that he learns that boys can be *ballerinos,* "the word for men."

Brandenberg, Alexa. *Ballerina Flying*. HarperCollins, 2002.

Mina and her ballet classmates demonstrate different aspects of ballet. They start with warm-ups and move on to the five positions. They do their exercises at the barre, including plié, tendu, and grand battement. They further demonstrate relevé, arabesque, pirouette, jeté, and when the class is over, révérence.

Brisson, Pat. *Tap-Dance Fever*. Illustrated by Nancy Cote. Boyds Mill, 2005.

Annabelle Applegate loves to tap dance. The adults in her rural community try to thwart her from dancing so much. Her dancing overcomes their efforts. Annabelle teaches some rattlesnakes to dance, and the townsfolk find a new appreciation for her art.

Brown, Margaret Wise. *Sailor Boy Jig*. Illustrated by Dan Andreasen. Margaret K. McElderry, 2002.

A sailor dog grabs a fishing pole and dances aboard a boat. He catches a fish and puts it in a fish bowl, dancing the entire time. He dances while preparing his meal of beans. And when he goes to sleep, his "jig is up!"

Burgard, Anna Marlis. *Flying Feet: A Story of Irish Dance*. Illustrated by Leighanne Dees. Chronicle, 2005.

Two young men arrive in the village of Ballyconnely at the exact same moment, both determined to become the new dancing master. They have a magnificent dancing competition, with Aidan Delaney winning by dancing on a cottage rooftop.

Burleigh, Robert. *Lookin' for Bird in the Big City*. Illustrated by Marek Los. Harcourt, 2001.

This is a fictionalized account of young jazz musician Miles Davis leaving his home in East St. Louis and looking for Charlie "Bird" Parker in New York City. When they finally meet up, Parker invites Davis onstage with him and tells him to take a solo.

Campbell, Bebe Moore. *Stompin' at the Savoy*. Illustrated by Richard Yarde. Philomel, 2006.

Mindy enjoys dancing but not in front of strangers at a recital. A talking drum takes her to the Savoy Ballroom. She sees Ella Fitzgerald, Chick Webb, and Benny Goodman perform as well as several dancing couples. She is inspired to dance herself and go with her aunts to the recital.

Carlson, Nancy. *Harriet's Recital.* Carolrhoda, 1982.

Harriet loves ballet class but hates recitals. She worries that she'll trip and fall or that her costume will rip. Onstage, she takes several deep breaths, takes a few steps, "and then . . . she was dancing!" She tells her parents afterward that she wasn't a bit frightened.

Cooper, Elisha. *Dance!* Greenwillow, 2001.

Tiny drawings show how dancers prepare their bodies and rehearse for a show. They meet in a dance studio and work with the choreographer. Musicians join the practices. Meanwhile, preparations are being made at the theater. Finally, the curtains go up.

Coulman, Valerie. *I Am a Ballerina.* Illustrated by Sandra Lamb. Lobster Press, 2004.

The young narrator wants to be a ballerina. She practices at home, sometimes knocking things over. Her father suggests that she take ballet lesson. She is persistent and has a wonderful time at the big recital.

Crimi, Carolyn. *Tessa's Tip-Tapping Toes.* Illustrated by Marsha Gray Carrington. Orchard, 2002.

Tessa the mouse "was built to dance." Instead of scurrying around the house in search for food like the other mice, Tessa straps on bottle-cap slippers and dances all night. When a singing cat arrives in the house, the two animals dance and sing all night long.

Cronin, Doreen. *Wiggle.* Illustrated by Scott Menchin. Atheneum, 2005.

A dog shows off a variety of ways to wiggle, including wiggling your tail and hair. The dog also wiggles with gorillas, fish, a crocodile, bees, polar bears, snakes, and birds. After wiggling with the moon, the dog runs out of wiggles and goes to bed.

dePaola, Tomie. *Oliver Button Is a Sissy.* Harcourt, 1979.

Oliver is teased and called a sissy. He dances at a local talent show and shines but doesn't win. When he gets to school the next day, however, he sees that someone has written on the wall "Oliver Button Is a Star."

Dillon, Leo and Diane. *Rap a Tap Tap: Here's Bojangles—Think of That!* Scholastic, 2002.

The Dillons celebrate the art of Bill "Bojangles" Robinson, acknowledged by many as the greatest tap dancer of all time. Bojangles is seen dancing in the street past a variety of people before finally dancing in formal attire on the theater stage.

Doyle, Malachy. *The Dancing Tiger*. Illustrated by Steve Johnson and Lou Fancher. Viking, 2005.

A little girl discovers a tiger dancing in the woods under the full moon. He allows her to dance with him during the different seasons. When the girl grows old, she helps her great-grandchild to take her place dancing with the tiger.

Durango, Julia. *Cha-Cha Chimps*. Illustrated by Eleanor Taylor. Simon & Schuster, 2006.

Ten little chimps sneak out one night and dance the cha-cha at Mambo Jamba's. One by one, they are joined by other animals to do other dances until Mama Chimp arrives. She takes them home, puts them to bed, calls a babysitter, and dances the cha-cha at Mambo Jamba's herself.

Edwards, Pamela Duncan. *Honk! The Story of a Prima Swanerina*. Illustrated by Henry Cole. Hyperion, 1998.

Mimi the swan is repeatedly chased out of the Opera House. She sneaks in through the stage door and follows several ballerinas onstage. She dances perfectly and is the hit of the evening.

Gauch, Patricia Lee. *Dance, Tanya*. Illustrated by Satomi Ichikawa. Philomel, 1989.

Little Tanya loves to dance with her older sister, Elise, but she's sad that she's too little to take dance lessons. After Elise's spring dance recital, Tanya performs her own dance in the family living room. Other Tanya books include

Bravo, Tanya (1992)

Tanya and Emily in a Dance for Two (1994)

Tanya and the Magic Wardrobe (1997)

Tanya and the Red Shoes (2002)

Gollub, Matthew. *Gobble, Quack, Moon*. Illustrated by Judy Love. Tortuga Press, 2002.

When Katie the cow expresses a desire to go into outer space, the other farm animals build a rocket ship. They dance on the moon but miss their home and Farmer Beth.

Graves, Keith. *Frank Was a Monster Who Wanted to Dance*. Chronicle, 1999.

Frank the monster puts live ants in his pants, heads for a local theater and dances for an appreciative audience. The theatergoers are distraught, however, when Frank's brains fall out of his head. They rush out of the theater as Frank loses more and more body parts. His unattached head brags, "Man can I dance!"

Gray, Libba Moore. *My Mama Had a Dancing Heart.* Illustrated by Raúl Colón. Orchard, 1995.

A mother and her daughter celebrate the changing seasons through dance. Spring features a flower-opening dance, while summer's dance splashes through waves. Autumn's ballet has leaf kicking, and winter finds the two dancing in slow motion with mittens and galoshes.

Hager, Sarah. *Dancing Matilda.* Illustrated by Kelly Murphy. HarperCollins, 2005.

Matilda the kangaroo dances from morning to evening—even in her dreams. This lively text is fun to read aloud. (I counted seventy-eight variations of the word *dance.*)

Hampshire, Susan. *Rosie's Ballet Slippers.* Illustrated by Maria Teresa Meloni. HarperCollins, 1996.

Rosie attends her first ballet lesson. Her teacher, called Madame, puts colored stickers on the dancer's heels to help them learn the proper moves. At the end of the class, Madame encourages the children to practice until they meet again.

Havill, Juanita. *Brianna, Jamaica, and the Dance of Spring.* Illustrated by Anne Sibley O'Brien. Houghton Mifflin, 2002.

Brianna and Jamaica are disappointed that they are flowers in the upcoming Dance of Spring and not the butterfly queen. When Nikki, the butterfly queen, is sick, Brianna gets a chance to play the role. When Brianna gets sick, they miss the performance but put on their own show in their living room.

Heidbreder, Robert. *Drumheller Dinosaur Dance.* Illustrated by Bill Slavin and Esperança Melo. Kids Can Press, 2004.

Several dinosaur bones have been found in Drumheller, Alberta, Canada. Some of the Drumheller dinosaur bones are featured in this story about dinosaur bones reassembling themselves and dancing. When nighttime ends, the dinosaurs "creep to their beds, unsnap tired bones and bury sleepy heads."

Hesse, Karen. *Come on, Rain!* Illustrated by Jon Muth. Scholastic, 1999.

A young girl sees some distant clouds during a hot, dry summer. She's optimistic and tells her friends to put on their bathing suits. When the rain comes down, the girls play in the rain. Their mothers join the girls, and "we grab the hands of our mammas. / We twirl and sway them, tromping through the puddles, romping and reeling in the moisty green air."

Hoff, Syd. *Oliver.* HarperCollins, 1960.

Oliver the elephant has trouble fitting in. The circus ordered ten elephants, and Oliver makes eleven. The zoo isn't looking for a new elephant, and everyone else already has a pet. Not until Oliver starts dancing does the circus regret its decision not to hire Oliver. The circus owner exclaims, "That's the best dancing elephant I've ever seen."

Holabird, Katherine. *Angelina Ballerina.* Illustrated by Helen Craig. Viking, 1983.

Angelina wants to do nothing but dance all day. Her family and friends are frustrated by her dance obsession. She's finally enrolled in a dancing school and starts to help around the house. We learn that after years of practice, she becomes the famous ballerina Mademoiselle Angelina. There are more than three dozen Angelina books and DVDs in this popular series.

Hurd, Edith Thacher. *I Dance in My Red Pajamas.* Illustrated by Emily Arnold McCully. HarperCollins, 1982.

Jenny loves to visit her grandparents. They play a whirling game, build a cat house, and make a blueberry pie. After her bath, Jenny puts on her red pajamas and dances with Grandpa, while Granny plays the piano and calls the dance. They agree that they all had "a beautiful, lovely, noisy day."

Isadora, Rachel. *Lili at Ballet.* Putnam, 1993.

Lili loves everything about the ballet. We follow her and her classmates as they stretch and practice their steps. We learn about the special shoes ballet dancers wear and different classes for boys. At the dance recital, Lili plays the part of a flower fairy.

Isadora, Rachel. *Max.* Macmillan, 1976.

Max is a great baseball player. One day, he watches his sister's dance class and decides to join in. He has fun and now uses dance class as a good way to warm up before his baseball games.

Isadora, Rachel. *Not Just Tights.* Putnam, 2003.

Young voices express the fears and the joys of putting on a ballet show. Practice takes a lot of hard work and pain. Other dancers make it look easy. When the show starts, dancers worry about stage fright, hitting their cues, having to go to the bathroom, and losing their tights. The applause makes it all worth it.

Isadora, Rachel. *On Your Toes: A Ballet ABC.* Greenwillow, 2003.

A is for *arabesque*, a dance pose. *B* is for *backstage*. *C* is for *costume*, and so on through *X* for "X Marks the Spot," *Y* for *yarn* to make leg warmers, and *Z* for *zipper*—needed for quick costume changes.

Jonas, Ann. *Color Dance*. Greenwillow, 1989.

Three young girls perform a dance that shows how colors mix to make new colors. Near the end of the dance, they are joined by a young man carrying a white, then gray, and finally a black cloth.

Kerins, Tony. *Little Clancy's New Drum*. Candlewick, 1996.

Clancy the turtle bangs on his drums and disturbs the other animals. The animals take away a succession of instruments. Clancy eventually cries so loudly that the other animals not only give him his instruments back but they also join him.

Kinert, Robert. *Clorinda*. Illustrated by Steven Kellogg. Simon & Schuster, 2003.

Clorinda the cow loves to dance, and she leaves the farm for the big city. She gets her chance to dance ballet but squishes her dancing partner. Nonetheless, the audience applauds, but she misses her home. She heads home and trains the other animals—and the farmer—to dance.

King, Stephen Michael. *Milli, Jack, and the Dancing Cat*. Philomel, 2003.

Jack and Cat wander into town and need new boots from Milli the shoemaker. Since they are broke, they promise to teach Milli how to dance instead. Milli makes her new friends new and wonderful shoes, instruments, and clothes.

Lasky, Kathryn. *Starring Lucille*. Illustrated by Marilyn Hafner. Knopf, 2001.

Lucille gets a tutu for her birthday. She's inspired to practice twirls, leaps, and jumps—and "a new way to hop." She even practices her curtsies. She gives a winning performance for her family and earns new admiration from her teasing brother.

Leiner, Katherine. *Mama Does the Mambo*. Illustrated by Edel Rodriquez. Hyperion, 2001.

Sofia wants to see her Mama dance again, but Mama hasn't danced since Papa died. Family friends conspire to find a new dancing partner for Mama. At the carnival, it's Sophie who turns out to be Mama's new dancing partner.

Lewison, Wendy Cheyette. *I Wear My Tutu Everywhere!* Illustrated by Mary Morgan. Grosset and Dunlap, 1996.

Tilly loves to dance all day long. She gets a pink tutu for her birthday and wears it everywhere—the supermarket, a hayride, the zoo (she "jeté-ed for the giraffes"), school, the pool, the train, in the rain, at the playground, and, of course, dancing class.

Littlesugar, Amy. *Marie in Fourth Position*. Illustrated by Ian Schoenherr. Philomel, 1996.

Marie is not a very strong dancer. To help make ends meet, she poses for the famous artist Monsieur Degas. Degas is very demanding on his models, making them pose for hours. The famous sculpture *The Little Dancer* is the result of their collaboration.

Marshall, James. *Swine Lake*. Illustrated by Maurice Sendak. HarperCollins, 1999.

A hungry wolf excitedly sees "well-dressed hogs" entering the theater to see a performance of *Swine Lake*. The wolf sneaks in and tries to decide which of the pig dancers to eat first. He gets so caught up in the ballet's story that he forgets all about his hunger.

Martin, Bill, and John Archambault. *Barn Dance!* Illustrated by Ted Rand. Holt, 1986.

A farm kid witnesses the scarecrow playing a fiddle and leading the farm and woodland animals into the barn for a big dance. A crow calls the dance. "Mules to the center for a curtsey an' a bow / An' hey there, skinny kid! Show the old cow how!"

Martin, Bill, and Michael Sampson. *Rock It, Sock It, Number Line*. Illustrated by Heather Cahoon. Holt, 2001.

The different numbers grab a variety of fruits and vegetables and dance around the garden. They dance before the king and queen (a boy and a girl) and end up as vegetable soup.

Mathers, Petra. *Sophie and Lou*. HarperCollins, 1991.

Sophie is a shy mouse. When a dance studio opens next door, she listens to the dance instructors through her window. She follows their instructions in the privacy of her own house. A gentleman caller named Lou rings her doorbell and asks her to dance.

Maybarduk, Linda. *James the Dancing Dog*. Illustrated by Gillian Johnson. Tundra, 2004.

James the dog enjoys spending time at the ballet company's studio. He is upset when a wolfhound is brought in to play a hunting dog for a performance of *Giselle*. James saves the day with "a soaring grand jeté" when the wolfhound gets stage fright.

Mayer, Marianna. *The Twelve Dancing Princesses.* Illustrated by K. Y. Craft. Morrow, 1989.

The king wonders why his daughters' dancing slippers are worn out each night. The young gardener Peter follows the princesses and learns that they head to a twilight kingdom each night and dance under a magic spell.

McCoy, Karen Kawamoto. *Bon Odori Dancer.* Illustrated by Carolina Yao. Polychrome, 1998.

Keiko is trying to perform her dance correctly for the Obon festival. She keeps crashing into the other girls. Day by day, the other girls help her learn the proper moves, and they are a hit at the festival.

McKissack, Patricia. *Mirandy and Brother Wind.* Illustrated by Jerry Pinkney. Knopf, 1988.

Mirandy captures Brother Wind and traps him in the barn. At a dance, she commands Brother Wind to help her and her friend Ezel to prance "'round and 'round, cutting corners with style and grace."

McMullan, Kate. *Noel the First.* Illustrated by Jim McMullan. HarperCollins, 1996.

Noel has the first-place position at the barre, and she's glad to be the class leader. She loses her spot to a couple of newcomers. Noel works harder and performs a piece from *Cinderella,* causing the dance teacher to exclaim, "This . . . is dancing!"

Medearis, Angela Shelf. *Dancing with the Indians.* Illustrated by Samuel Byrd. Holiday House, 1991.

A rural African American family drive their wagon to visit the Seminole Indians. They watch the Ribbon Dance, a rattlesnake dance, and dances that tell stories of ancient battles. At the break of day, the family is invited to join the Indian Stomp Dance.

Michelson, Richard. *Happy Feet: The Savoy Ballroom, Lindy Hoppers and Me.* Illustrated by E. B. Lewis. Harcourt, 2005.

A young boy's father owns Pop's Shoeshine Shop in Harlem. Happy Feet, as the boy is called, hears stories of the day he was born, which coincided with the opening of the Savoy Ballroom in Harlem across the street.

Mitton, Tony. *Dinosaurumpus!* Illustrated by Guy Parker-Rees. Orchard, 2002.

The dinosaurs rush down to dance "near the sludgy old swamp." They're all frightened by the appearance of the tyrannosaurus, but he only wants to join in the dance. Soon, "everybody's doing the dinosaur romp."

Mitton, Tony. *Down by the Cool of the Pool*. Illustrated by Guy Parker-Rees. Orchard, 2001.

A frog encourages a duck, pig, sheep, cat, dog, goat, pony, donkey, and cow to dance with him by the pool. They all crash into each other and into the water. "They splished and splashed till their dance was done."

Newsome, Jill. *Dream Dancer*. Illustrated by Claudio Muñoz. HarperCollins, 2001.

Lily loves to dance. Unfortunately, she injures herself and must wear a cast. She buys a ballerina doll that she is able to pose into different positions. Lily is nervous when she rejoins her dance class but gains confidence through her doll.

Patrick, Denise Lewis. *Red Dancing Shoes*. Illustrated by James E. Ransome. Morrow, 1993.

The narrator receives "a pair of the finest, reddest, shiniest shoes that anyone had ever seen." She's sad when the shoes get dirty, but Nen, her aunt, cleans them good as new. "'It's magic, Nen!' I said. 'No,' she laughed, 'just a little wash and polish.'"

Pinkwater, Daniel. *Dancing Larry*. Illustrated by Jill Pinkney. Marshall Cavendish, 2006.

Larry the polar bear starts dance lessons until he is told by Madame Swoboda that polar bears may not dance. Little Mildred Frobisher teaches Larry some ballet moves, and he, in turn, teaches them to other polar bears. They all perform a ballet version of "Goldilocks and the Three Bears" and invite Madame Swoboda.

Puttock, Simon. *A Ladder to the Stars*. Illustrated by Alison Joy. Holt, 2001.

A young girl wishes upon a star that she could dance with it. The star hears the girl and arranges to have a special seed planted in the girl's garden. It takes years and years for a tree to grow as high as the sun. The girl is now an old woman, but she successfully climbs the tree and dances with the star.

Roberts, Brenda C. *Jazzy Miz Mozetta*. Illustrated by Frank Morrison. Farrar, Straus and Giroux, 2004.

Miz Mozetta gets all dressed up for an evening of dancing, but her elderly friends complain that their dancing days are over. She goes sadly back to her apartment. Her older friends cheer her up by donning their old dancing clothes and dancing the jitterbug in her living room. They even invite the young folks to learn the dance moves.

Ryder, Joanne. *Big Bear Ball*. Illustrated by Steven Kellogg. HarperCollins, 2002.

Bears arrive from all over, including on hot-air balloons, to dance at the Big Bear Ball. The dance procession heads to the water, where the bears tussle with an alligator. The dance ends as morning arrives.

Ryder, Joanne. *Dance by the Light of the Moon*. Illustrated by Guy Francis. Houghton Mifflin, 2007.

Buffalo Flo, Gertie May Goose, Cassie Sue Cat, and Patty Ann Pig dress up and go to the evening dance. They meet up with their dancing partners at Farmer Snow's farm and "dance by the light of the moon."

Samuels, Barbara. *Dolores on Her Toes*. Farrar, Straus and Giroux, 2003.

The day before Tutu Day, Dolores dresses her cat Duncan up in a tutu and twirls him around the room. He escapes through an open door. Dolores looks everywhere in vain, although the reader is able to spot Duncan. To find Duncan, Dolores dresses and acts like a cat.

Schaefer, Carole Lexa. *Dragon Dancing*. Illustrated by Pierr Morgan. Viking, 2007.

Mei Lin and her classmates create a dancing birthday dragon out of crafts. They imagine the dragon dancing out of the classroom and through imaginary settings until the teacher calls them all back in for snacks.

Schroeder, Alan. *Ragtime Tumpie*. Illustrated by Bernie Fuchs. Little, Brown, 1989.

A young girl named Tumpie dances to ragtime music whenever she has a chance. She wins a local dance contest in the early 1900s and earns a silver dollar. The story is based on the life of performer Josephine Baker.

Schubert, Leda. *Ballet of the Elephants*. Illustrated by Robert Andrew Parker. Roaring Brook Press, 2006.

The true story of Stravinsky's composition "Circus Polka" is detailed from conception through performance. Circus-owner John Ringling North, choreographer George Balanchine, and others worked with Stravinsky to develop a dance for real elephants.

Shannon, George. *Dance Away*. Illustrated by Jose Aruego and Ariane Dewey. Greenwillow, 1982.

Rabbit loves to dance. "Left two three kick, right two three kick." A hungry fox captures Rabbit's friends. Rabbit saves them with his special dance and sends Fox flying "into the cold river water."

Sis, Peter. *Ballerina!* **Greenwillow, 2001.**

While a little girl practices ballet in front of her mirror, the reader learns several dance expressions, such as stretch, twirl, leap, tiptoe, reach, dip, flutter, and float. With her colorful costumes and props, and her great imagination, she "is the best ballerina of all."

Smith, Cynthia Leitich. *Jingle Dancer.* **Illustrated by Cornelius Van Wright and Ying-Hwa Hu. Morrow, 2000.**

Jenna wants to dance at the next powwow. She practices by watching a video of her grandmother jingle dancing. She borrows some jingles from her relatives and friends and adds them to her dance regalia. She proudly dances for the women in her life.

Stadler, Alexander. *Lila Bloom.* **Farrar, Straus and Giroux, 2003.**

Lila is tired of ballet lessons. Madame Vera tells Lila that she's dancing like an old noodle. Lila is embarrassed and dances her best for the rest of the lesson. As she dances, Lila gets happier and decides to take "two classes a week instead of one."

Stanley, Mandy. *Lettice the Dancing Rabbit.* **Simon & Schuster, 2001.**

A rabbit hops into the city and joins a ballet class. Her bunny friends watch her perform and then head back to the countryside. Lettice misses being a rabbit and decides "being a rabbit was, by far, the very best thing in the world."

Stevenson, James. *Flying Feet.* **Greenwillow, 2004.**

Tap-dancers Tonya and Ted offer dance lessons for the residents of Mud Flats. The first practice is a disaster. Stan helps put on a show when Tonya and Ted turn out to be crooks who leave in the middle of the night.

Stower, Adam. *Two Left Feet.* **Bloomsbury, 2004.**

Rufus is a monster who loves to dance, but he has two left feet—literally. He enters a dance contest with a young monster named Maddie, and they win by dancing in perfect harmony. We learn at the end of the book that Maddie has two right feet.

Sweeney, Joan. *Bijou, Bonbon and Beau: The Kittens Who Danced for Degas.* **Illustrated by Leslie Wu. Chronicle, 1998.**

Three kittens and their mother take up residence in a ballet theater in Paris. They become favorites of the dancers, crew, and the local artist, Degas. When the kittens run onstage during a performance, they become a hit with the audience.

Taylor, Ann. *Baby Dance*. Illustrated by Marjorie van Heerden. HarperCollins, 1999.

A father swings his baby daughter back and forth and up and down while Mama is napping on the couch. The book starts with the lines "Hush little baby, don't you cry."

Wallace, Ian. *Chin Chiang and the Dragon's Dance*. Atheneum, 1984.

Chin Chiang is excited but also nervous about dancing with his grandfather in the dragon dance. He meets a woman who used to dance the dragon dance. Together, they conquer their fears and take up the dragon's tail "while the throngs of people cheered them on."

Walsh, Ellen Stoll. *Hop Jump*. Harcourt, 1993.

All frogs hop and jump. Betsy tries dancing instead. When she's told that there's no room for dancing, she finds her own space. Soon, the other frogs join her and decide there's "no room for hopping." Betsy tells them that there's room for both.

Walton, Rick. *How Can You Dance?* Illustrated by Ana López-Escrivá. Putnam, 2001.

Walton instructs children to dance in a variety of ways. Dance like a frog by pulling arms and legs in and pushing them out. Dance like the trees by waving your arms wildly. The last dance is a good-bye dance.

Wheeler, Lisa. *Hokey Pokey: Another Prickly Love Story*. Illustrated by Janie Bynum. Little, Brown, 2006.

Cushion the porcupine wants to learn to dance. His quills and clumsiness get in the way as he tries to learn the fox-trot from a fox, the bunny hop from a rabbit, and the funky chicken from a hen. Barb the hedgehog teaches Cushion all of those dances, plus the hokey pokey.

Wilson, Karma. *Hilda Must Be Dancing*. Illustrated by Suzanne Watts. Margaret K. McElderry, 2004.

When Hilda danced, "the jungle floor would shake and quake." The other animals ask her to take up knitting instead, but she quickly returns to dancing. When the water buffalo suggests that she take up swimming, Hilda discovers the joy of water ballet.

Winthrop, Elizabeth. *Dumpy La Rue*. Illustrated by Betsy Lewin. Holt, 2001.

Dumpy, a pig, wants to dance but is told that pigs don't dance. "They bellow, they swallow, they learn how to wallow." Dumpy ignores his parents and dances for the farm animals. All of the farm animals, in turn, are inspired to dance along with Dumpy.

Wood, Audrey. *Little Penguin's Tale.* **Harcourt, 1989.**

Grand Nanny Penguin tells a cautionary tale about Little Penguin, who comes across some dancing gooney birds. After dancing and acting wild at the Walrus Polar Club, Little Penguin falls asleep by the sea and is eaten by a whale. Grand Nanny Penguin's young charges are horrified, so she provides a happier ending for Little Penguin.

Young, Amy. *Belinda the Ballerina.* **Viking, 2002.**

Belinda's feet are very, very big—too big for a ballerina. Dejected, Belinda gets a job as a waitress at Fred's Fine Food. She dances for the customers and becomes a local hit. The maestro at the ballet discovers her, and Belinda becomes an even bigger star. Sequels published by Viking include

Belinda and the Glass Slipper (2006)

Belinda in Paris (2005)

Resources

Many of the recordings in this book can be found at many major online bookstores, such as Amazon.com and Barnesandnoble.com. The following websites also carry many of the recordings found in this book:

CD Baby: www.cdbaby.com

KiddoMusic: www.kiddomusic.com

North Side Music: www.northsidemusicwi.com

Songs for Teaching: www.songsforteaching.com

Online services such as iTunes (www.itunes.com) and Bill Shontz's Children's Music Hall of Fame (http://www.billshontz.com/cmhof.html) feature downloads of several recordings found in this book.

The following companies handle a set roster of recording artists:

Casablanca Kids: www.casablancakids.com

A Gentle Wind: www.gentlewind.com

Music for Little People: www.musicforlittlepeople.com

Putumayo Kids: http://www.putumayo.com/playground.html

Rounder Kids: www.rounderkids.com

Individual Artist Websites

Many artists have their own websites. In most cases, you can purchase their products directly from these websites or, sometimes, you will be directed to a vendor that carries their products. As of the writing of this book, the following artists have websites that contain ordering information:

Abell, Timmy: www.timmyabell.com

Allard, Peter and Ellen: www.peterandellen.com

Alsop, Peter: www.peteralsop.com

Avni, Fran: www.franavni.com

Banana Slug String Band: www.bananaslugstringband.com

Barchas, Sarah: www.highhavenmusic.com

Bartels, Joanie: www.joaniebartels.com

Beall, Pamela, and Susan Nipp: www.weesing.com

Berkner, Laurie: www.twotomatoes.com

Big Jeff: www.bigjeffmusic.com

Boynton, Sandra: www.sandraboynton.com

Byers, Kathy: www.kathybyers.com

Cassidy, Nancy: www.nancycassidymusic.com

Chapin, Tom: http://members.aol.com/chapinfo/tc/

Charette, Rick: http://www.pinepoint.com/rick.html

The Chenille Sisters: www.cantoorecords.com

Coffey, James: www.jamescoffey.com

Colleen and Uncle Squaty: http://colleenandunclesquaty.com

Cosgrove, Jim: www.jimcosgrove.com

Craig n Co.: www.craignco.com

Crow, Dan: www.dancrow.com

Daddy A Go Go: www.daddyagogo.com

Dana: www.swiggleditties.com

Del Bianco, Lou: www.findlou.com

Diamond, Charlotte: www.charlottediamond.com

Feldman, Jean: www.drjean.org

Fink, Cathy, and Marcy Marxer: www.cathymarcy.com

Fite, Stephen: www.melodyhousemusic.com

Foote, Norman: www.normanfoote.com

Frezza, Rebecca: www.bigtruckmusic.com

Gemini: www.geminichildrensmusic.com

Gill, Jim: www.jimgill.com

Grammer, Red: www.redgrammer.com

Green Chili Jam Band: http://kumo.swcp.com/kidzmusic/

Greg and Steve: www.gregandsteve.com

Grunsky, Jack: www.jackgrunsky.com

Harley, Bill: www.billharley.com

Harper, Jessica: www.jessicaharper.com

Harper, Monty: www.montyharper.com

Haynes, Sammie: www.sammiehaynes.com

Hinojosa, Tish: www.mundotish.com

Howdy, Buck: www.buckhowdy.com

Hullabaloo: www.hullabalooband.com

Jenkins, Ella: www.ellajenkins.com

Jonas, Billy: www.billyjonas.com

Kaldor, Connie: www.conniekaldor.com

Kaye, Mary: www.marykayemusic.com

Kimmy Schwimmy: www.kimmyschwimmy.com

Kinder, Brian: www.kindersongs.com

Kinnoin, Dave: www.songwizard.com

Kirk, John, and Trish Miller: www.johnandtrish.com

Knight, Tom: www.tomknight.com

LaFond, Lois: www.loislafond.com

The Learning Station: www.learningstationmusic.com

John Lithgow: www.johnlithgow.com

Bob Livingston: www.texasmusic.org

Ken Lonnquist: www.kenland.com

Madsen, Gunnar: www.gunnarmadsen.com

Marxer, Marcy: www.cathymarcy.com

Mayer, Hans: www.hansmayer.com

McCutcheon, John: www.folkmusic.com

McDermott, Joe: www.joemcdermottmusic.com

McGrath, Bob: www.bobmcgrath.com

McMahon, Elizabeth: www.mrsmcpuppet.com

Milkshake: www.milkshakemusic.com

Miss Amy: www.missamykids.com

Mitchell, Elizabeth: www.youaremyflower.org

Moo, Anna: www.annamoo.com

Mr. Al: www.mralmusic.com

Muldaur, Maria: www.mariamuldaur.com

Nagler, Eric: www.ericnagler.com

Ode, Eric: www.ericode.com

Old Town School of Folk Music: www.oldtownschool.org

Palmer, Hap: www.happalmer.com

Parachute Express: www.parachuteexpress.com

Paxton, Tom: www.tompaxton.com

Pease, Tom: www.tompease.com

Penner, Fred: www.fredpenner.com

Peterson, Carole: www.macaronisoup.com

Pirtle, Sarah: www.sarahpirtle.com

Polisar, Barry Louis: www.barrylou.com

Pullara, Steve: www.coolbeansmusic.com

Raffi: www.raffinews.com

Ralph's World: www.ralphsworld.com

Raven, Nancy: www.lizardsrockmusic.com

Riders in the Sky: www.ridersinthesky.com

Roberts, Justin: www.justinroberts.org

Rosen, Gary: www.garyrosenkidsmusic.com

Rosenthal, Phil: www.americanmelody.com

Roth, Kevin: www.kevinrothmusic.com

Rudnick, Ben: www.benrudnickandfriends.com

Rymer, Brady: www.bradyrymer.com

Sharon, Lois, and Bram: www.casablancakids.com

Shontz, Bill: www.billshontz.com

Silberg, "Miss Jackie": www.jackiesilberg.com

Simmons, Al: www.alsimmons.com

Sprout, Jonathan: www.jonsprout.com

Staines, Bill: http://www.acousticmusic.com/staines/

SteveSongs: www.stevesongs.com

Stotts, Stuart: www.stuartstotts.com

Sweet Honey in the Rock: www.sweethoney.com

Thaddeus Rex: www.thaddeusrex.com

They Might Be Giants: www.tmbg.com

Tickle Tune Typhoon: www.tickletunetyphoon.com

Trout Fishing in America: www.troutmusic.com

Tucker, Nancy: www.nancytucker.biz

Vitamin L: www.vitaminl.org

Walker, Graham: www.grahamwalker.ca

Yosi: www.yosimusic.com

Zanes, Dan: www.danzanes.com

Index

Note: Song titles are in quotation marks; book titles are italic.

B

Rob Reid is a full-time instructor at the University of Wisconsin–Eau Claire specializing in children's literature and literature for adolescents. He is the author of several ALA Editions books, including *Family Storytime; Something Funny Happened at the Library; Cool Story Programs for the School-Age Crowd; Children's Jukebox;* and *Children's Jukebox,* second edition. He is a regular contributor to *Book Links* magazine and *LibrarySparks* magazine, and he has an online column for the Children's Literature Network titled Heart of a Child. He is a recent recipient of the Wisconsin Librarian of the Year. In addition to teaching and writing, Reid visits schools and libraries as a children's humorist, using storytelling, musical activities, and wordplay to make reading come alive for children.